PAGE PUBLISHING
Conneaut Lake, PA

First originally published by Page Publishing 2023

ISBN 978-1-6624-6536-9 (pbk)
ISBN 978-1-6624-6537-6 (digital)
ISBN 979-8-88793-706-9 (hardcover)

Printed in the United States of America

ON A BRISK AUTUMN MORNING, TRAVALE TREMONT AND HIS CLASSMATES/NEIGHBORHOOD FRIENDS ARE ABOUT TO EMBARK ON SOMETHING MORE THAN A SLAVE SHIP, MORE THAN A FIELDTRIP; IN FACT, THEY ARE DESCENDING ONTO SOMETHING MUCH, MUCH MORE...

WHILE HIS NEIGHBORHOOD FRIEND AND CLASSMATE, REGINA, PERUSED OVER THE SIDE RAILS, EYES GLAZED WITH DISBELIEF FROM THE HORRID SLAVE TALES, STEPHANIE, HIS GIRLFRIEND, MENTALLY ABSORBS THE ANGUISH THE SLAVES SUFFERED THROUGH HER FINGERTIPS FROM THE LASHES LEFT ON THE WHIPPING POST. TRAVALE CURIOUSLY WANDERS OFF.

SO DAT'S A REAL LIVE SLAVE SHIP UHH? COLD-BLOODED MAN!

MS. LOCKHART AND HER JIVE FIELDTRIPS. DIS IS GONNA BE A DRAG MAN.

RIGHT ON! THIS IS GONNA BLOW MY BUZZ MAN.

THEM SLAVERY DAYS WUZ SHO'NUFF MESSED UP. JIVE CAN SLAVE-TRADERS.

MAN, EVEN THE WOOD GOT TORN BY THE WHIPS. HEAVY MAN HEAVY!

YES, ON THIS GLOOMY GRAY, 1978 MORNING, THIS NORTHWESTERN HIGH JUNIOR DISCOVERS A TREASURE OF AGONY, WITH A MEASURE OF INFAMY, THAT ONLY A FEW GREAT MORTALS HAVE KNOWN OF ONLY IN FANTASY, THUS IT'LL BECOME HIS REALITY.

MS. LOCKHART, TRIPPIN' OUT! SOME NEWLY RENOVATED SLAVE SHIP. WIT A BIG OL' HOLE IN THE FLOOR. MAN, SUMTHIN' REAL FUNKY DOWN THERE!

TRAVALE DOESN'T NOTICE THE "DO NOT ENTER" SIGN THAT HAS BEEN BLOWN DOWN, AND HE DOESN'T KNOW HOW FRAGILE THE WOOD THAT SUPPORTED HIS WEIGHT WAS AND, LIKEWISE, NEITHER DOES HIS TEACHER, OR HIS CLASSMATES KNOW OF HIS WHEREABOUTS OR OF HIS FATAL FALL, AND NOW...

AAGH! THE WOOD BROKE STEPHA—

HAVING FALLEN INTO THE CRACK OF AN OLD SLAVE SHIP ON A HIGH SCHOOL FIELD TRIP, TRAVALE TREMONT'S HEART IS THRUST THROUGH WITH THE SHAFT OF AN ANCIENT AFRICAN KING'S ONCE POWERFUL STAFF WHICH WAS ENDOWED WITH MAGICAL INCANTATIONS. THIS FATAL ACCIDENT IS ON THE 600TH ANNIVERSARY OF THE DEATHS OF OVER 200 CAPTURED SLAVES, ALL OF WHICH DIED TOGETHER HORRIBLY.

THE BLOOD FROM HIS DEATH AWAKENS THE SPIRITS CONFINED WITHIN THE WALLS OF THE CARGO AREA. THEY AWAKE TO INHABIT HIS BODY—MIGHTY WARRIORS, WARLORDS, WARLOCKS, WITCHDOCTORS, AND THE HEART OF THE MOST POWERFUL MAJESTIC KING, WHOSE BODY WAS SLAIN CEREMONIOUSLY BEFORE SUBORDINATES. TREMONT'S LIFELESS BODY LIES ONLY AS A GHOSTLY SHELL, SWAPPING PLACES WITH THE DEAD. NOW, THE DEAD ARISE IN HIM TO LIVE OUT THEIR PURPOSE AND CONQUER THEIR ENEMIES—ANY AND ALL ENEMIES OF

BLACKMAN!

MEANWHILE, MANY MILES DEEP BENEATH THE OCEAN FLOOR, WHILE THE CLASS EXPEDITION WAS STILL IN ITS PLANNING PHASE, COLOSSAL, CITY-SIZED BOULDERS SHIFTED, AND UNDERWATER CREATURES OOZED THROUGH THE CRACKED EARTH.

UNLEASHING UNBRIDLED, UNKNOWN EVIL TO THE WORLD ABOVE IT, FORCING THEIR WORLDS TO COLLIDE.

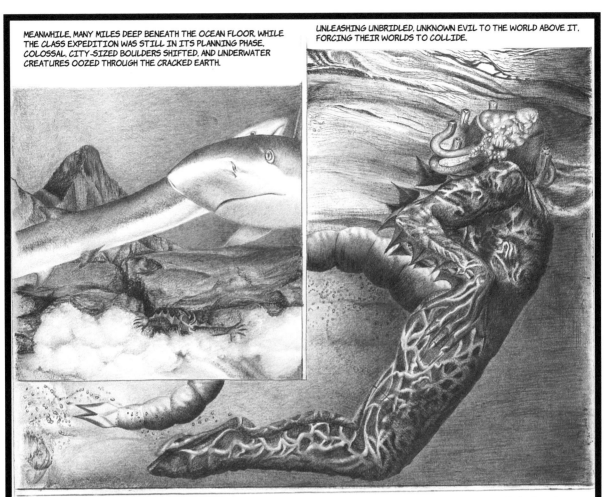

AND NOW, HUNDREDS OF MILES IN THE ATLANTIC OCEAN, LITERALLY ON THE OTHER SIDE OF THE WORLD, A SINISTER EVIL DESCENDS ON AN UNSUSPECTING VICTIM AS IT EMERGES.

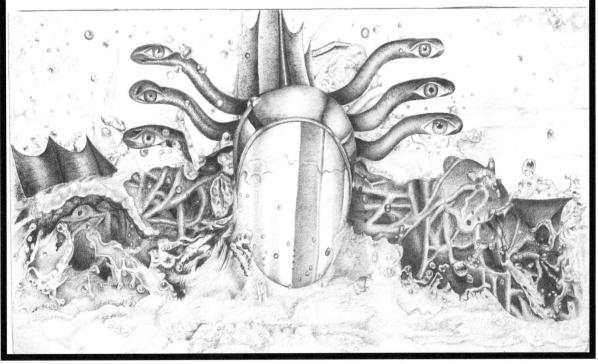

FROM THE LOWEST DEPTHS AND THE BOWELS OF THE ABYSS ARISES AN UNKNOWN CREATURE OF THE DARKNESS THAT SLITHERED, THEN BURSTS ITS WAY THROUGH GIGANTIC SLABS OF EARTH THAT SHUFFLED AT THE PLANET'S CORE, CAUSING EARTHQUAKES, FLOODS, AND UNTOLD DEATHS, SECRETLY HERALDING THE TUMULTUOUS ARRIVAL OF...

AND NOW, AFTER HAVING WROUGHT HAVOC BEHIND IT AMONG THE SEAS IN ITS WAKE AND HAVING CONSUMED NUMEROUS SOULS, ITS INSATIABLE APPETITE HAS YET TO BE APPEASED. NOR CAN IT BE. THE SLAVE SHIP WITH STUDENTS STATIONED ALONGSIDE OF VIRGINIA KEY BEACH IS A FEAST OF SOULS, BECKONING HIS LUST FOR DEATH TOWARD IT. HE RAPIDLY APPROACHES BEHIND A BLANKET OF IGNORANCE AS THE TEENAGERS UNWARILY JEST ABOUT HIS MURDEROUS DESCENT.

HEY, STEPH! I MUST BE BUGGIN', BUT WHAT'S DAT OVER THERE?

I DON'T KNOW, GIRL. IT LOOKS LIKE A MAN ON A KITE.

REGINA'S FRIVOLITY REFLECTS THE MOOD OF THE SCHOOL OUTING, WHICH ONLY ALLOWS THE CREATURE—SOON TO BE KNOWN AS VEIN—TO HAVE THE TIME TO EMBARK BEFORE THEY CAN FLEE. MEANWHILE, ALL THIS IS TAKING PLACE WHILE TRAVALE IS BELOW DECK AND THE 600-YEAR-OLD SPELL IS TAKING EFFECT.

MS. LOCKHART AND DEM A TRIP. WHATEVER IT IS, IT'S UGLY AS HELL. I'M GONNA SUE THEM FOR PUPIL ABUSE. GET IT? I'M A PUPIL/EYE PUPIL," REGINA SAYS AS SHE GIGGLES.

CHILD, PLEASE! GIRL, YOU ARE BUGGIN'! DAT WUZ SO DRY!

AND NOW, IT IS SUDDENLY ABOARD, UNLEASHING ITS DEADLY FUMES THAT EMIT FROM ITS VENOMOUS VEINS, LETHAL BLACK TOXINS THAT SHRED SOULS FROM THE LIVING TO BE FED TO IT: SOULS THAT BECOME SPOILS OF ITS DIRECT ATTACK!

AND THE VIOLENT CARNAGE ENSUES...

STEPH, DON'T GO OVER THERE! THOSE THINGS...THEY KILLIN' PEOPLE!

LET GO! TRAV, JUST WENT THAT WAY! TRAV! OH MY GOD! TRAV!

TRAVALE TREMONT, THE PREEMINENT EMBODIMENT OF CENTURIES OF THE BLACKMAN, NOW ARISES FROM THE CAULDRON, WHICH WAS A TOMB FOR THE JUST PREYED ON BY THE UNJUST, PREPARED TO EXACT THEIR VENGEANCE. UPON HEARING THE CALL OF HIS DEAREST LOVE, STEPHANIE, HE ERUPTS! THEN BECOMES A PRIMARY SOURCE TO FEED UPON TO VEIN DUE TO THE COLLECTIVE SOULS HIS BODY ENCASES, AND THUS A RIVALRY OF THE AGES EMERGES.

I'M COMING, STEPH! WHERE YA AT!

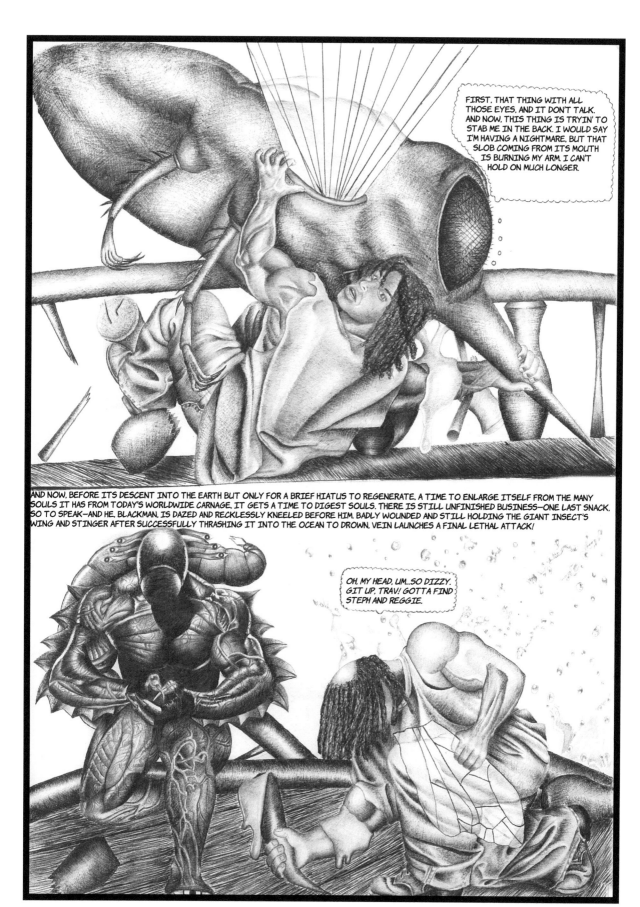

FIRST, THAT THING WITH ALL THOSE EYES, AND IT DON'T TALK. AND NOW, THIS THING IS TRYIN' TO STAB ME IN THE BACK. I WOULD SAY I'M HAVING A NIGHTMARE, BUT THAT SLOB COMING FROM ITS MOUTH IS BURNING MY ARM. I CAN'T HOLD ON MUCH LONGER.

AND NOW, BEFORE ITS DESCENT INTO THE EARTH BUT ONLY FOR A BRIEF HIATUS TO REGENERATE, A TIME TO ENLARGE ITSELF FROM THE MANY SOULS IT HAS FROM TODAY'S WORLDWIDE CARNAGE, IT GETS A TIME TO DIGEST SOULS. THERE IS STILL UNFINISHED BUSINESS—ONE LAST SNACK, SO TO SPEAK—AND HE, BLACKMAN, IS DAZED AND RECKLESSLY KNEELED BEFORE HIM. BADLY WOUNDED AND STILL HOLDING THE GIANT INSECT'S WING AND STINGER AFTER SUCCESSFULLY THRASHING IT INTO THE OCEAN TO DROWN, VEIN LAUNCHES A FINAL LETHAL ATTACK!

OH, MY HEAD, UM...SO DIZZY. GIT UP, TRAV! GOTTA FIND STEPH AND REGGIE.

8

SUDDENLY AND INSTINCTIVELY, OUR WOUNDED WARRIOR LEAPS, ESCAPING CERTAIN DISMEMBERMENT BY VEIN'S RAZOR SHARP POISONOUS INJECTORS AT THE END OF HIS TAIL, AN ANCIENT ALLOY OF UNKNOWN METALS HARDENED BY CENTURIES OF INHERENT ADAPTION TO THE HEAT AT THE CORE OF THE EARTH; ANOTHER ASPECT OF ITS MURDEROUS ARSENAL. THE VOICELESS VILLAIN GIVES NO WARNING SOUNDS, ONLY A STENCH FROM ITS TOXIC FUMES WHEN SECRETED.

I THOUGHT YOU SPLIT SLICK. NOW, I GOTTA SOCK IT TO YOU, AND DAT'S GROOVY, BABY.

MAN, THIS IS BABBID. I HIT THAT DUDE WIT ALL I HAD. I CAN'T LET THAT TAIL HIT ME. THEN WHAT NEXT?

ALAS, THE LEAP SEVERELY EXPOSES THE NEWFOUND YOUNG PRINCE, WHO MISJUDGED THE MONSTER'S QUICKNESS, TO A MORBID COCKTAIL WITHIN THE VEINS OF VEIN. A THREE-HEARTED DEATH MACHINE, ALL OF WHICH PUMP OUT DIFFERENT LEVELS OF TOXINS; GREEN BLOOD, WHICH RENDERS ONE IN A PERMANENT CATATONIC STATE—ALIVE YET NO VITAL SIGNS—RED BLOOD, A LENGTHY SLOW VIOLENT DEATH, AND BLACK BLOOD, DEATH WITHIN SECONDS. THERE IS NO EARTHLY CURE AMONG BLOOD TYPES, AND VEIN HAS ELECTED TO SLICE INTO BLACKMAN WITH THE DEADLIEST DOSE, WHICH SECRETES THROUGH HIS VEINS FROM HIS KNIFELIKE CLAWS INTO HIS BELLY.

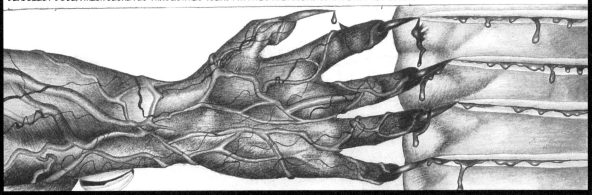

AND OFF IN THE DISTANCE BEFORE VEIN CAN TOLL THE MANY SOULS INSIDE OF BLACKMAN, THEN SINK BACK INTO THE DEPTHS OF THE EARTH, A STRANGE FORM IS DESCENDING TOWARD THE MELEE, SOMETHING HALF-WOMAN, HALF-BEAST, AND ALL EVIL. AND SHE IS DRAWN TO SADNESS, DRAWN TO CONFUSION. SHE IS ANOTHER REFUGEE FROM DEEP WITHIN THE ABYSS. THE FRIGHTENED PEOPLE THINK SHE IS BATTLING THE MONSTER FOR THEIR SAKES. THEIR TRUST IS MISPLACED. SHE IS BATTLING FOR A VICTIM TO TORTURE.

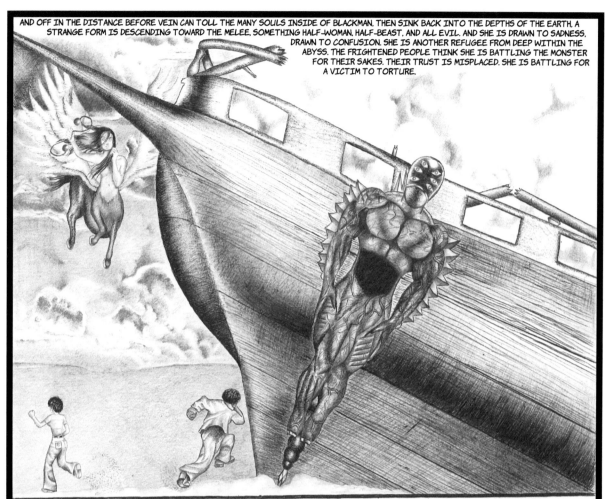

MEANWHILE, BACK ON BOARD THE SHIP, TRAVALE'S LIFELESS BODY LIES STILL WITH HIS HEAD CRADLED IN THE LAP OF HIS GIRLFRIEND OF TWO YEARS, STEPHANIE. HER AND REGINA SURVIVED THE ONSLAUGHT OF HORROR, ONLY TO BE FACED WITH THE TRAGEDY OF THE DEATH OF THEIR BEST FRIEND AND RESCUER ON THIS HIGH SCHOOL FIELDTRIP GONE AWRY. WHILE IN THE BACKGROUND, EXPLOSIVES BURST LOUDER THAN THEIR SCREAMS FOR HELP, THE BLASTS IN THE SAND FROM THE CONFRONTATION BETWEEN THE TWO VILLAINS IS DEAFENING—THE SOUNDS THAT SIGNAL THE ARRIVAL OF AMUK!

HELP US! PLEASE! SOMEBODY HELP!

DON'T DIE ON ME, BABY. COME ON, BABY. I KNOW YOU CAN HEAR ME. GIT UP, TRAV. WHAT AM I GONNA DO WITHOUT YOU? GIT UP, POOCHIE. REGGIE, I'M NOT GETTING A PULSE!

OH MY GOD! HE'S DYIN'! HELP! HELP! SOMEBODY PLEASE, HELP US!

AND NOW AS BLACKMAN STILL LIES DYING, AND AS VEIN SINKS BENEATH THE EARTH, BEWILDERED FROM NOT BEING ABLE TO HAVE TAKEN THE SOULS OF BLACKMAN, AND AMUK HAVING HAD BOMBARDED VEIN WITH HER EXPLOSIVES, THE SCREAMS IN THE BACKGROUND OF MS. LOCKHART BEING TAKEN BY AMUK TO BE TORTURED ARE MUFFLED OUT. BUT THE FAINT WHISPERS OF LOVE FROM STEPHANIE CALLING ON TRAV'S HEART, THE MEMORIES AND THE FLASHBACKS BEGIN TO PLAYBACK INTO HIS MIND, BACK INTO A TIME AT THE BEGINNING WHEN THEY FIRST MET. IN THIS HIS SECOND STAGE OF DEATH, LIKE THE FIRST, HE HEARS ONLY HER VOICE AND SEES ONLY HER FACE. AND HER FIRST WORDS TO HIM WERE...

11

AND STILL TODAY, LIKE THE FIRST DAY THEIR EYES MET IN CHEMISTRY CLASS, THEIR LOVE HASN'T CHANGED. BUT STEPHANIE CHAVEZ DOESN'T REALIZE THAT THE DEAD DON'T DIE, AND NEITHER DOES OUR YOUNG PRINCE KNOW OF HIS NEWFOUND IMMORTALITY. AND LIKE THEIR IMMORTAL LOVE, HE ARISES FROM THE WRECKAGE THROUGH THE WHISPERED WORDS SIMILAR TO THAT VERY DAY. THE CURIOUS CHILDLIKE WORDS WITH A MATURE INSIGHT, THINKING HER FRIEND IS DYING, THINKING HER FRIEND IS GONE, SHE ASKED...

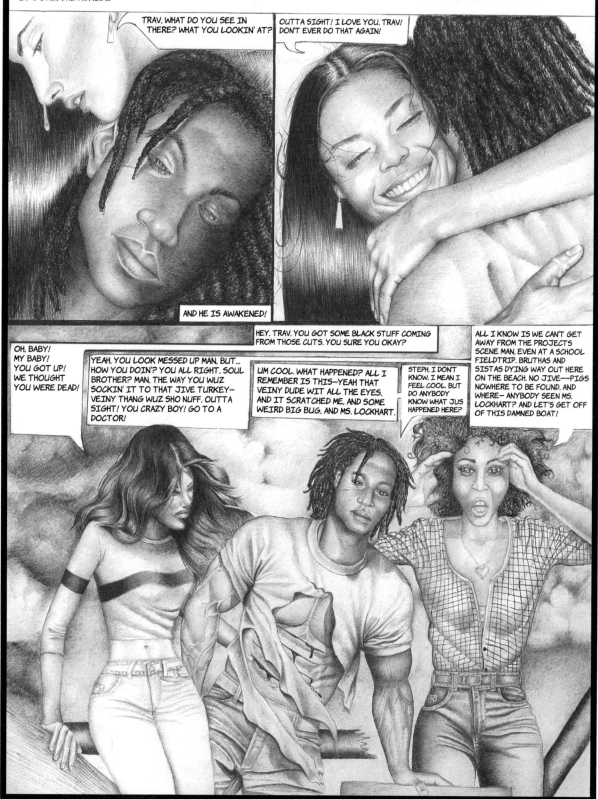

TRAV, WHAT DO YOU SEE IN THERE? WHAT YOU LOOKIN' AT?

OUTTA SIGHT! I LOVE YOU, TRAV! DON'T EVER DO THAT AGAIN!

AND HE IS AWAKENED!

HEY, TRAV, YOU GOT SOME BLACK STUFF COMING FROM THOSE CUTS. YOU SURE YOU OKAY?

OH, BABY! MY BABY! YOU GOT UP! WE THOUGHT YOU WERE DEAD!

YEAH, YOU LOOK MESSED UP MAN, BUT... HOW YOU DOIN'? YOU ALL RIGHT, SOUL BROTHER? MAN, THE WAY YOU WUZ SOCKIN' IT TO THAT JIVE TURKEY—VEINY THANG WUZ SHO NUFF, OUTTA SIGHT! YOU CRAZY BOY! GO TO A DOCTOR!

UM COOL. WHAT HAPPENED? ALL I REMEMBER IS THIS—YEAH THAT VEINY DUDE WIT ALL THE EYES, AND IT SCRATCHED ME, AND SOME WEIRD BIG BUG, AND MS. LOCKHART.

STEPH, I DON'T KNOW. I MEAN I FEEL COOL, BUT DO ANYBODY KNOW WHAT JUS HAPPENED HERE?

ALL I KNOW IS WE CAN'T GET AWAY FROM THE PROJECTS SCENE MAN, EVEN AT A SCHOOL FIELDTRIP. BRUTHAS AND SISTAS DYING WAY OUT HERE ON THE BEACH. NO JIVE——PIGS NOWHERE TO BE FOUND, AND WHERE— ANYBODY SEEN MS. LOCKHART? AND LET'S GET OFF OF THIS DAMNED BOAT!

AS DEADLY AS SHE IS BEAUTIFUL, SHE LAMENTS AS SHE KILLS. THE MORE SHE MOURNS, THE GREATER THE PAIN SHE INFLICTS. SHE BRINGS AN ENDLESS SEA OF TEARS, WHILE HER CALMNESS CAUSES ONE TO GO...

13

THE ASSAULT FROM THE BELLY OF THE OCEAN NOW HAVING ENDED, A NEW GHASTLY CHAPTER COMMENCES. A SIDE ROAD TO TERROR WHERE THE LOUDEST SCREAMS YIELD MORE JOY TO AMUK!

PLEASE LADY...UH...MS. HORSE THANG? WHATEVER YOU ARE, PLEASE PUT ME DOWN? WHERE ARE YOU TAKING ME?

YOU MUST RELAX, MY DEAR. SOON YOU WILL BE EXPERIENCING EXQUISITE PAIN. YOU WILL BE IN A DRUNKEN HAZE OF PURE AGONY. SOON YOU WILL STAND ON THE THRESHOLD BETWIXT LIFE AND DEATH. TENSING YOUR BODY MUSCLES IN SUCH A WAY WILL ONLY DESTROY THE BEAUTY OF THE CARVINGS I INTEND TO CUT INTO YOUR FLESH.

I DON'T KNOW YOU, AND YOU DON'T KNOW ME. WHY DO YOU WANT TO HURT ME? I THOUGHT YOU WERE RESCUING US FROM THAT VEINY THANG?

HUSH, ROBUST ONE. YOU ARE STIRRING UP THE ACIDS. IT DOESN'T MIX WELL WITH SERRATED SKIN. BESIDES, YOUR PUREST SCREECHES MUST BE PRESERVED FOR MY CRESCENDO.

LIKE A BEAST HIDDEN IN THE SHADOWS TO DEVOUR ITS PREY, AMUCK ARRIVES AT AN ISOLATED FAR OFF OF THE MIAMI COASTLINE AND SLAYS THE ISLAND HOPPING COUPLE THERE, BEFRIENDS THEIR DOGS, AND PREPARES TO TORMENT MS. LOCKHART, HER SELECT CHOICE VICTIM, AFTER WHICH, SHE WILL FULFILL HER PROMISE TO HER FOUR—LEGGED BROTHERS TO FEED THEM THE SWEET FLESH OF FEAR OF THE TWO—LEGGED ONES THAT SHE WILL CUT BONES FROM AND PARTAKE IN AS SHE LAMENTS IN HER VICTIM'S PAIN.

UGH, IT—UGH—STANDS FOR PEACE... PLEASE, PLEASE DON'T KILL ME?

YOU TWO—LEGGED ONES HAVE ALWAYS HAD LOFTY GOALS. HOW CAN YOU EVER HAVE PEACE IF YOU WON'T SUCCUMB TO THE DARKNESS INSIDE EACH OF YOU? SUBMIT, ROBUST ONE. SUBMIT TO THE LIBERATING PAIN AND ITS BOUNDLESS ENERGY. ENJOY THE SADNESS, THE SWEETNESS IN EVERY TEARDROP.

THE MAHABHARATA, I KNOW. BUT WHAT IS THIS SYMBOL?

THE DEPTHS OF YOUR ANGUISH FEEL SO INTENSE, SO INTOXICATING, SO RAW. OH, I CRY FOR YOU.

15

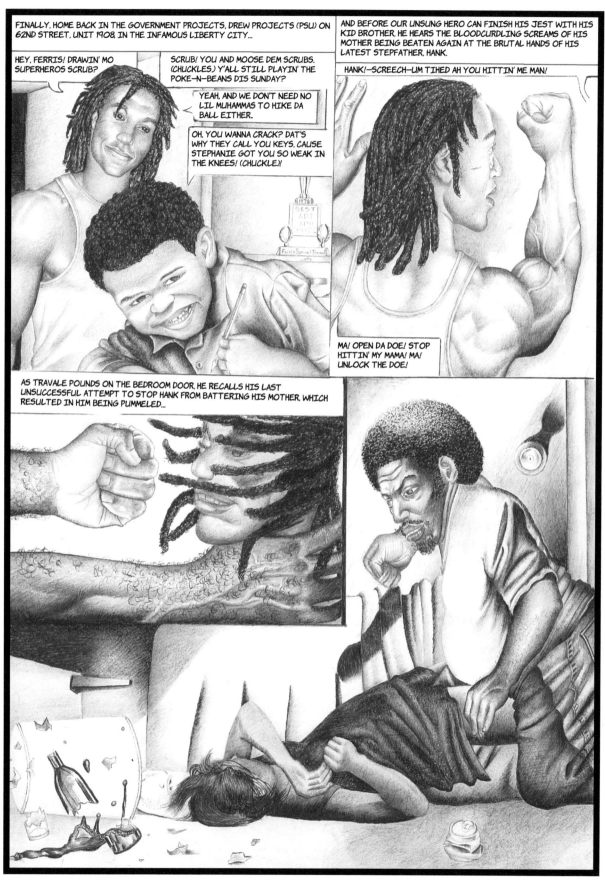

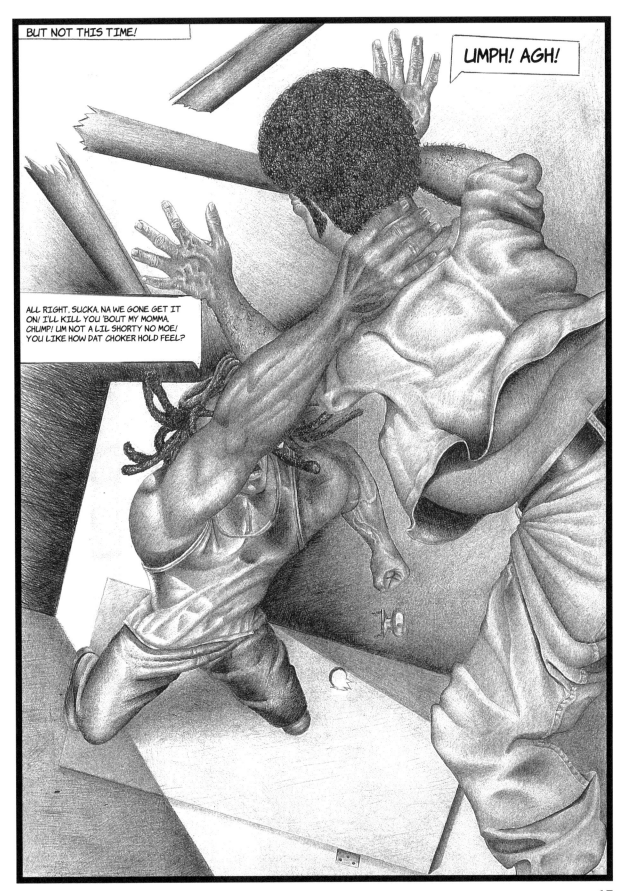

17

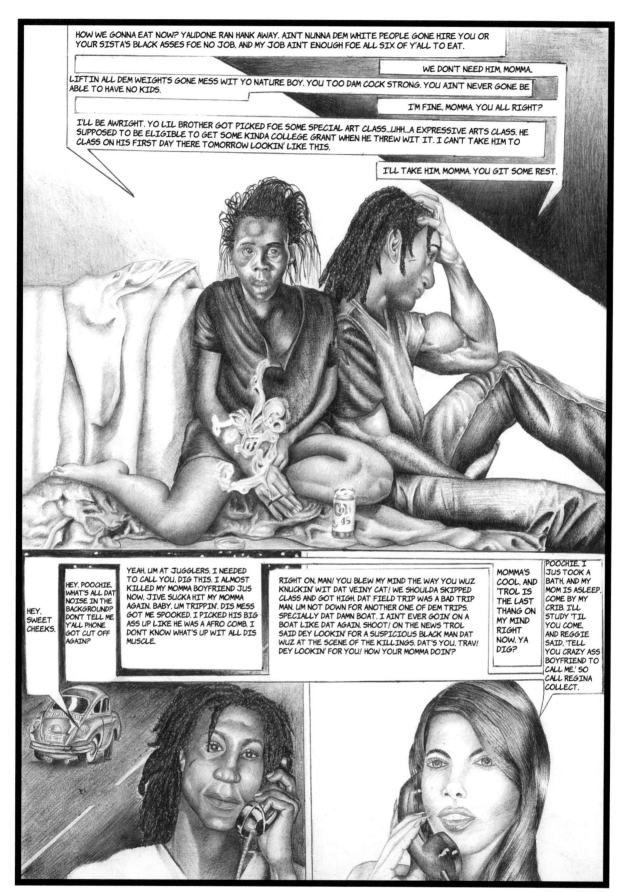

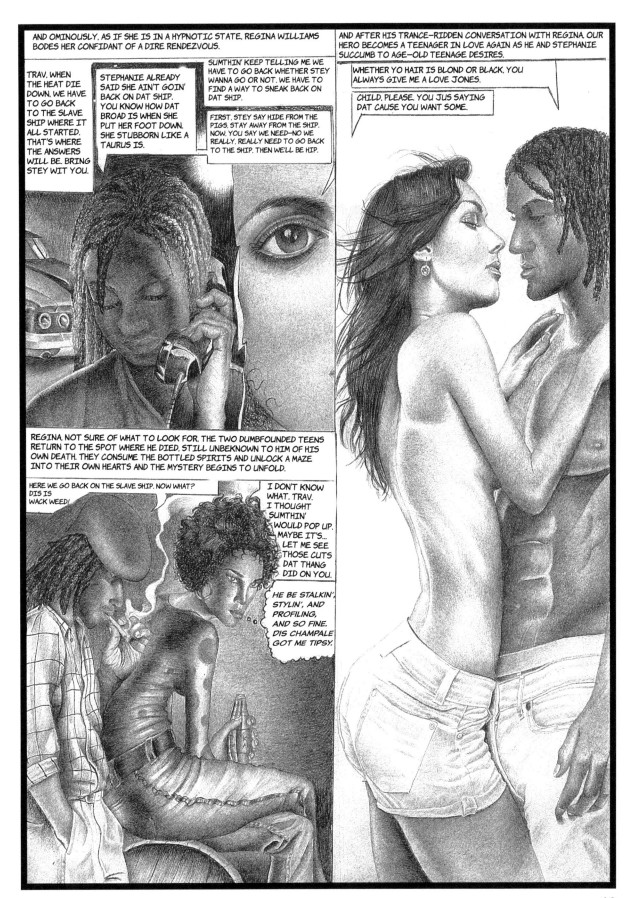

19

DOWN IN THE HULL OF THE SLAVE SHIP, APTLY NAMED JUNTAMENTE, TRAVALE AND REGINA WALK DANGEROUSLY, STRADDLING THAT THIN LINE OF FRIENDSHIP AND LOVERS. MAYBE IT'S TEENAGE HORMONES, MAYBE IT IS NATURAL, BUT WHAT COMES NEXT IS A BAD IDEA. OR IS IT?

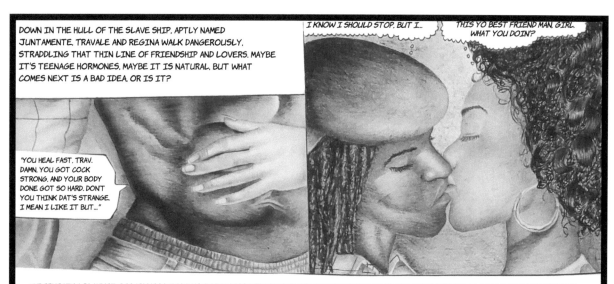

UNDERNEATH A BLANKET OF DARKNESS, THE TWO TEENAGERS MERGE INTO ONE: DRAWN TOGETHER BY A HIDDEN ATTRACTION. OR COULD IT BE A PUPPET MASTER CALLED FATE, THAT DREW THEM TOGETHER? BY USING THE ABSOLUTE SECRECY OF SECLUSION TO REVEAL ITS TRIUMPHS, TRAGEDIES, AND PURPOSE TO THEM. A REVELATION OF THE AGES.

UNDERNEATH THE CLOAK OF DARKNESS, ASTOUNDING THINGS HAVE OCCURRED. YES, AT TIMES, EVEN DARKNESS HAS BEEN A VEHICLE FOR LIGHT. QUASI, IN THIS CASE DARKNESS, IS PARTNERED WITH FATE TO ENLIGHTEN AS A SILENT TEARDROP FALLS QUIETLY IN THE SHADOW. THE SCALES THEN FALL FROM THE TEENAGER'S EYES AS REGINA'S GENETIC CODE MERGES GENTLY WITH THE 600-YEAR-OLD BLOODLETTING OF HER ANCESTORS, WHILE SHE LEANS FAITHFULLY ATOP THE LOCATION WHERE HER ANCESTORS DIED CEREMONIOUSLY IN A SELF-INFLICTED SACRIFICIAL RITUALISTIC CARNAGE 600 YEARS AGO. THE MIGHTY WARRIORS, FEARLESS WITCHDOCTORS OF BLACK MAGIC, THE KING WITH HIS ENTOURAGE, AND THE EXACT SPOT WHERE TRAV DIED AND WAS INHABITED BY THEM AND THUS WAS REVIVED BY THEIR SOULS.

WHAT ABOUT STEPHANIE? SHE TOLD ME DAT ALL SHE EVER THINK ABOUT IS YOU, AND WE DOWN HERE, BONING AND GETTIN' IT ON IN THE DARK. MAN, DIS WUZ COLD-BLOODED.

DIG DIS, IT AIN'T RIGHT, BUT IT AIN'T WRONG EITHER. I MEAN, WE CAN'T HELP WHAT WE FEEL.

JUS DON'T TELL STEPHANIE.

21

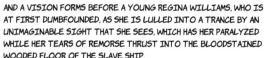

AND A VISION FORMS BEFORE A YOUNG REGINA WILLIAMS, WHO IS AT FIRST DUMBFOUNDED, AS SHE IS LULLED INTO A TRANCE BY AN UNIMAGINABLE SIGHT THAT SHE SEES, WHICH HAS HER PARALYZED WHILE HER TEARS OF REMORSE THRUST INTO THE BLOODSTAINED WOODED FLOOR OF THE SLAVE SHIP.

SHE SEES BACK TO THE BEGINNING, OVER 600 YEARS AGO. THE DESPERATE DEDICATION OF A QUEEN, PERILOUSLY ANXIOUS TO SAVE THE LIVES OF HER PEOPLE WHO WERE DYING IN BATTLE AND FROM SICKNESS.

A QUEEN WHO HEARD OF A MYTHICAL TREE CALLED THE TREE OF LIFE, WHICH WAS BEING GUARDED BY CHERUBIM NEAR THE GIHON RIVER IN THE LAND OF ETHIOPIA. SURELY, SHE THOUGHT THESE CHERUBIM, IF THEY EXIST, WERE NO MATCH FOR HER FINEST WARRIORS—WARRIORS WHO WERE EXCELLENT MARKSMEN, SWIFT AFOOT WITH UNPARALLELED STRENGTH. THEY WERE SOLDIERS WHO SEEMINGLY CHEATED EVEN THE DEATH ANGEL THAT FELL ON HER VILLAGE. SHE THOUGHT, *IF ONLY I COULD POSSESS THIS "TREE OF LIFE," MY NATION WOULD NOT PERISH.* SHE THOUGHT WRONG.

23

YET UNFORTUNATELY, SHE WAS CORRECT, CONCERNING THE TREE OF LIFE, FOR THE MYTH TURNED OUT TO BE TRUE. SHE DISCOVERED THE LOCATION OF THE TREE OF LIFE, AND THE PRICE OF HER DISCOVERY WAS THE LIVES OF HER REMAINING PEOPLE. ALAS, AS SHE HERSELF, WHO WAS THE LAST TO DIE, LAY DYING WITH HER LAST GASP OF AIR. THE MASTER OF THE CHERUBIM GRANTED HER TO GRASP THE FRUIT OF THE TREE OF LIFE, FOR SHE FOUGHT IN THE MANNER OF THE WARLORDS OF OLD. A TIME BEFORE, TIME ITSELF WAS RECORDED, AND HE HAD RESPECT TOWARD HER.

AND THROUGH THE MERE TOUCH OF THE STRANGE CEREBRAL FRUIT OF THE TREE OF LIFE, SHE WAS ENDOWED TO BEHOLD ALL THE MYSTERIES OF THE ANCIENTS. THE QUEEN AND ALL THE KNOWLEDGE SHE HAD GAINED DIED WITH HER THAT DAY. THE TRUTH THAT WISDOM IS LIFE AND WITH THAT WISDOM, SHE KNEW THAT DEATH'S ARRIVAL WAS JUSTIFIED FOR A TIME, UPON TIME. UNTIL NOW THE SPIRIT OF QUEEN ITHALIA IS REINCARNATED INTO HER DEEP DESCENDANT DAUGHTER, REGINA, WHO NOW STANDS DUMBFOUNDED IN A STATE OF HYPNOSIS, PEERS DEEPLY THROUGH THE BEGINNING OF HER ANCESTORS' JOURNEY FROM FREEDOM, TO SLAVERY, TO FREEDOM, AS IT WERE.

SHE NEVER ACTED LIKE THIS BEFORE. WHAT WUZ IN DAT REEFER?

REGGIE! WHY YOU LOOKIN SO SPACEYEYED? YOU TRIPPIN OUT, REGGIE!

THEN SUDDENLY, REGINA TEMPORARILY TRANSFORMS AND COMBINES TO SHARE THE ESSENCE OF HER GREAT—GRANDMOTHER, QUEEN ITHALIA, BY TAKING HER PLACE TO THE RIGHT OF THE MIGHTY KING ÝTU WITH THE MAGICAL ROD THAT WAS GIVEN TO HIM BY THE OMNIPOTENT WITCHDOCTOR, ABIHU. SHE THEN ALLOWS TRAVALE TO LOOK BRIEFLY UPON THE VISION AND HEAR SACRED TRUTHS AS SHE OPENS HER MOUTH TO EXPLAIN THE SOURCE AND ORIGIN OF HIS MYSTERIOUS POWERS. SHE REVEALS THE INTERVENTION OF FATE, EVEN TO THE HOLE IN THE SLAVE SHIP ATOP THE WATER, PUSHED BY SLAIN SPIRITS AND HIS FATAL FALL ONTO THE BLOOD.

MANY GENERATIONS SEPARATE US, YET WE UNITE FOR ONE PURPOSE—TO REGAIN OUR FULL HONOR BY THE DEFEAT OF THOSE WHO SEEK OUR DEMISE, HOW BE IT IN THE FLESH, IN THE SPIRIT, OR IN THE MIND, AND WITH THIS ROD THEY WILL FALL. FOR THERE ARE THREE WHO BEAR WITNESS ON EARTH— THE SPIRIT, THE WATER, AND THE BLOOD. THESE THREE AGREE AS ONE. YOU ARE THE INEXTINGUISHABLE BLACKMAN FROM THE LINEAGE OF THE MIGHTY INDESTRUCTIBLE. HAIL, BLOOD BROTHER, TO THE SONS OF CHAOS. HAIL, HE WHO POSSESSES THE POWERFUL HEART OF KING ÝTU.

25

REGGIE! YOU COOL? YOU WUZ ZONKED OUT AND LOOKIN' INTO SPACE. THEN YOU CLICKED AND SHOWED UP LOOKIN' BADD IN THESE OUTTA SIGHT THREADS LIKE SOME FOXY AFRICAN QUEEN AND WUZ TALKIN' LIKE A SQUARE. YOU WUZ RAPPIN' SOME HEAVY LINES BOUT THIS SLAVE SHIP, THE JUNTAMENTE, THE TRIBE OF WARRIORS ON IT, SOME KING, AND SOME WIZ CAT. YO HAIR WUZ DID DIFFERENT, YOUR FACE WUZ THE SAME, BUT YOU SOUNDED ALL FUNNY.

TRAV, THAT WAS A VISION OF MY ANCIENT ANCESTOR, QUEEN ITHALIA. THROUGH HER EYES, I COULD SEE THE BEGINNING OF TIME AND THE SPIRIT WORLD. WHEN YOU FELL IN THE SHIP, THE SPIRITS PLANNED THAT TO COME INTO YOU. VEIN IS THE NAME OF DAT THING WIT NO FACE. IT SWALLOWS UP SOULS WHOLE AFTER THE POISON FROM HIS VEINS OR DAT THINK SMOKE RIP THE SOULS FROM DA BODIES IT WANT YOU THE MOST FOR ALL THE 300 WARRIOR SPIRITS YOU HAVE INSIDE YOU.

THE HALF-HORSE, HALF-LADY IS CALLED AMUK. DEY CAME FROM THE WORLD IN THE CENTER OF OUR WORLD. SHE FEED ON PAIN AND HUMAN FLESH. DEY WILL BE BACK. DEY CAN'T GET FULL 'CAUSE THEY COLD-BLOODED MAN, 'TIL DA DEATH. BUT THE STRENGTH OF 300 BAD AFRICAN WARRIORS IZ YO ENDLESS BLACK POWER, AND WIT THE HEART OF KING YTU, YO CHEST GOT HEART SOUL BROTHER, AND PLUS WIT DA COOL MAGIC OF ABIBU AND THE VOODOO IN HIS SLICK STICK, HIS MIND BLOWIN' MAGIC IZ DA BADDEST. ALTOGETHER WITH THEM, YOU WILL BE ABLE TO GET IT, ON WIT ANYBODY AND ANYTHING.

IT'Z FUNNY HOW ONE DAY, WE WUZ ALL BUMMED OUT AND TRIPPIN' BOUT A OL' WACK SCHOOL FIELD TRIP AND JUS LIKE DAT, HERE WE GO IN ALL DIS CRAZY JIVE. MAN, DIS IZ OUTTA SIGHT! RIGHT ON, BABY! I WOULD SAY IT'S THE REEFER AND CHAMPALE, BUT DAT WORE OFF A WHILE AGO.

I LOVE STEPH, EVERYBODY KNOW DAT, BUT WHAT ABOUT THE WAY REGINA JUS BLEW MY MIND? SHE A THOROUGHBRED TOO. MAN! I SHOULD BE THINKING 'BOUT FERRIS.

WE JUS STARTED ON A LONG TRIP, MAN. I HOPE YOU DOWN 'CAUSE WHEN IT COME, WE GONE HAVE TA KEEP ON TRUCKIN', TRAV. I GOTTA TELL YOU DAT EVEN THOUGH THE SPIRITS AIN'T NO LONGER BOUND TO DA SLAVE SHIP BUT INSIDE A YOU. DEY ONLY WIT YOU WHEN YOU RIGHT. BUT IF YOU WRONG, YOU WON'T HAVE SUPER BLACK POWER. SO, LIKE IF YOU GO FOR BAD, YOU ON YO OWN MAN. WE GOTTA SPLIT! YOUR LIL BROTHA IN TROUBLE!

I DON'T KNOW HOW TO TELL HIM, HE DIED DAT DEY ON THE SHIP, BUT HE GAVE ME A LOVE JONES WHEN WE GOT IT ON. FERRIS IZ IN BAD SHAPE, WE GOTTA HURRY!

HOW DO YOU KNOW? WHAT DID HE DO? WHAT'Z WRONG? WHERE IS MY BROTHER?

FERRIS IS IN THE HOSPITAL.

YOUR BROTHER IS GOING TO BE FINE. BUT WE WON'T BE ABLE TO SAVE HIS LEFT ARM I'M AFRAID WE'LL HAVE TO AMPUTATE IT. HIS ARM IS BEYOND REPAIR. I'M SORRY.

BUT, BUT DAT'Z HIS DRAWING HAND! DAT'S ALL HE EVER DO IZ DRAW AND TALK ABOUT ART! YOU GOTTA BE ABLE TO SAVE IT. YOU GOTTA! HOW HE GONNA DRAW?

DOCTOR, YOU SURE THAT THERE AIN'T NOTHING YOU CAN DO?

IF WE DON'T, THE INFECTION IN HIS OBLITERATED ARM WILL INVADE HIS BLOODSTREAM AND KILL HIM

DUZ ANYBODY KNOW FOR SURE WHAT HAPPENED?

ACCORDING TO OUR RECORDS, THEY INDICATE THAT IT WAS AN ACCIDENT...

WHILE REGINA TENDERLY BRUSHED HER HAND ACROSS FERRIS' LEG IN HIS UNCONSCIOUS STATE IN THE BED BEFORE THEM AT JACKSON HOSPITAL. BLACKMAN IS DAZED AFTER SWALLOWING HARD. THE BITTER NEWS THAT TASTE LIKE A GULP OF THREE 6S ON A HOT TIN SPOON. THEN STEPHANIE ALSO INTERROGATES THE SURGEON.

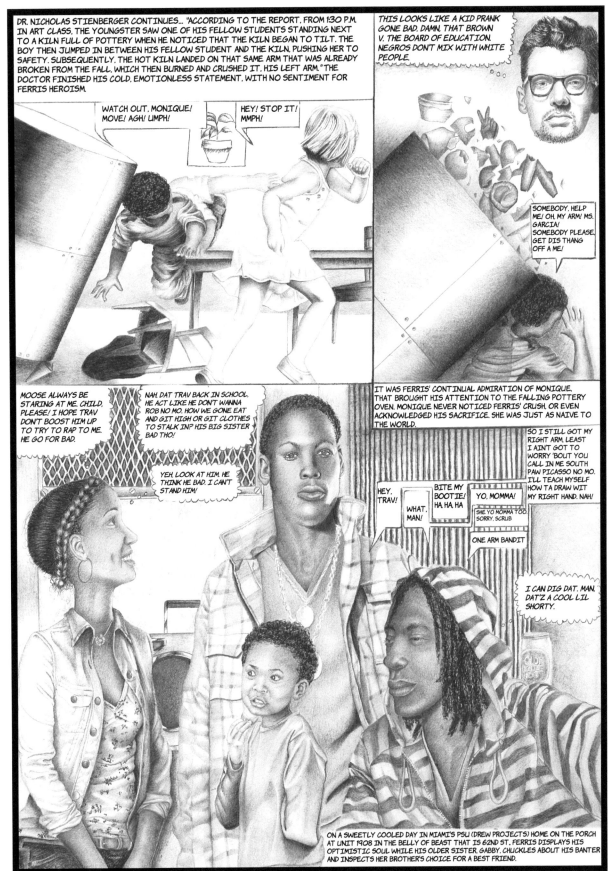

DR. NICHOLAS STIENBERGER CONTINUES... "ACCORDING TO THE REPORT, FROM 1:30 P.M. IN ART CLASS, THE YOUNGSTER SAW ONE OF HIS FELLOW STUDENTS STANDING NEXT TO A KILN FULL OF POTTERY WHEN HE NOTICED THAT THE KILN BEGAN TO TILT. THE BOY THEN JUMPED IN BETWEEN HIS FELLOW STUDENT AND THE KILN, PUSHING HER TO SAFETY. SUBSEQUENTLY, THE HOT KILN LANDED ON THAT SAME ARM THAT WAS ALREADY BROKEN FROM THE FALL, WHICH THEN BURNED AND CRUSHED IT, HIS LEFT ARM." THE DOCTOR FINISHED HIS COLD, EMOTIONLESS STATEMENT, WITH NO SENTIMENT FOR FERRIS HEROISM.

WATCH OUT, MONIQUE! MOVE! AGH! UMPH!

HEY! STOP IT! MMPH!

THIS LOOKS LIKE A KID PRANK GONE BAD. DAMN, THAT BROWN V. THE BOARD OF EDUCATION. NEGROS DON'T MIX WITH WHITE PEOPLE.

SOMEBODY, HELP ME! OH, MY ARM! MS. GARCIA! SOMEBODY PLEASE. GET DIS THANG OFF A ME!

MOOSE ALWAYS BE STARING AT ME, CHILD, PLEASE! I HOPE TRAV DON'T BOOST HIM UP TO TRY TO RAP TO ME. HE GO FOR BAD.

NAH, DAT TRAV BACK IN SCHOOL, HE ACT LIKE HE DON'T WANNA ROB NO MO. HOW WE GONE EAT AND GIT HIGH OR GIT CLOTHES TO STALK IN? HIS BIG SISTER BAD THO!

YEH, LOOK AT HIM. HE THINK HE BAD. I CAN'T STAND HIM!

IT WAS FERRIS' CONTINUAL ADMIRATION OF MONIQUE, THAT BROUGHT HIS ATTENTION TO THE FALLING POTTERY OVEN. MONIQUE NEVER NOTICED FERRIS' CRUSH, OR EVEN ACKNOWLEDGED HIS SACRIFICE. SHE WAS JUST AS NAIVE TO THE WORLD.

SO I STILL GOT MY RIGHT ARM LEAST I AIN'T GOT TO WORRY 'BOUT YOU CALL IN ME SOUTH PAW PICASSO NO MO. I'LL TEACH MYSELF HOW TA DRAW WIT MY RIGHT HAND. NAH!

HEY, TRAV!

WHAT, MAN!

BITE MY BOOTIE! HA, HA, HA

YO, MOMMA!

SHE YO MOMMA TOO. SORRY, SCRUB

ONE ARM BANDIT

I CAN DIG DAT, MAN, DAT'Z A COOL LIL SHORTY.

ON A SWEETLY COOLED DAY IN MIAMI'S PSU (DREW PROJECTS) HOME ON THE PORCH AT UNIT 1908 IN THE BELLY OF BEAST THAT IS 62ND ST, FERRIS DISPLAYS HIS OPTIMISTIC SOUL WHILE HIS OLDER SISTER GABBY, CHUCKLES ABOUT HIS BANTER AND INSPECTS HER BROTHER'S CHOICE FOR A BEST FRIEND.

27

AT NORTHWESTERN HIGH'S SATURDAY NIGHT DANCE, WITH THE SAWDUST STREWN ACROSS THE GYM FLOOR FOR BETTER DANCING SLIDING MOVES, THE GHETTO TEENS ATTEMPT TO ESCAPE THE RANCID ACIDIC TASTE THAT THEIR LIVES HAVE LEFT ON THEIR TONGUES AFTER PUSHING IT DOWN WITH CHEAP, ILLEGALLY-PURCHASED MALT LIQUOR AND MARIJUANA FOR CHASERS. FRY, THE SCHOOL BAND DIRECTOR, ALSO PLAYS AN OLD PAM GRIER FILM VIA A MOVIE PROJECTOR ON THE GYM WALL. OUR BELEAGUERED HERO CLUMSILY DANCES WITH HIS BELOVED, STEPHANIE, AMONG THEIR FRIENDS AND CLASSMATES.

HE ACTIN LIKE HE BOOGYING DOWN BACK THERE, LOOKIN' AT MY BUTT. HE ACT LIKE HE LIKE IT THO.

IT'Z A GOOD THANG I LOVE TRAV. HE DANCE SO AWKY, BUT HE DON'T GET IT ON LIKE DAT.

WHO IZ DAT WIT REGINA?

I HOPE DAT POPPIN' SOUND I HEAR IS THE SPEAKERS AND NOT SOME GUNSHOTS.

BUT HE STALKIN' IN THOSE KING THE TAILOR PANTS, HUH HUM.

LET ME SHOW DIS BRICK HOUSE DEEZ COLD MOVES!

HE FINE! BUT WHAT HE DOIN' WIT DAT WHITE GIRL IN HERE?"

28

LIKE THE FAMILIAR CHILL OF DEATH ON YET ANOTHER AWFULLY WARM FALL, MIAMI NIGHT IN THE FUNNY WEATHER CAPITOL OF THE WORLD. THE ALL-TOO-FREQUENT POPPING NOISE WHICH LAMBASTED, THEN ROASTED THE LOUD SPEAKERS INTO SUBMISSION, GIVING WAY TO A BULLET SEASONING OF DEATH ON THE HARDWOOD SERVED RAW, COLD, AND OVERFLOWING WITH A SIDE OF UNMEASURABLE MAUDLIN. THE PERFECT RECIPE FOR THE INSATIABLE APPETITE OF AMUK, WHO IS DRAWN TO MAYHEM AND GLOOM LIKE STENCH IS TO DECOMPOSITION. AS MOOSE AND GOOGOO BLASTING AIMLESSLY AT MUDDY EYE, SNOTBOX, AND DINOSAUR, WITH BULLETS STOPPING ANYWHERE AND IN ANYBODY, OUR YOUNG HERO'S DIRE SUSPICIONS BECAME UNWELCOMELY INVITED TO YET ANOTHER LIBERTY CITY HIGH SCHOOL DANCE SHOOTOUT COMMONALITY. OR IS IT?

AND OUTSIDE, AS TRAV SYSTEMATICALLY HAULED REGINA AND STEPHANIE TO SAFETY, THERE SHE STOOD, WEARING MS. LOCKHART'S NECKLACE THAT SHE WORE SO PROUDLY, GIVEN TO HER FROM HER STUDENTS. IT STRUCK HIM THEN THAT THIS HALF-HORSE, HALF-WOMAN CREATURE NOT ONLY ORCHESTRATED HER DISAPPEARANCE, BUT HAD KILLED MS. LOCKHART. THE VENGEANCE GORGED THROUGH HIS BODY. HIS EYES BURNED, SEETHING WITH THE TEARS OF A LION AS HE GLARED INTO HER SOULLESS, GLASSY, COLD STARE.

AND WITH COMPLETE RECKLESS ABANDON, BLACKMAN LEAPT, SURGING WITH ENRAGED FURY, TAKING NO THOUGHT FOR HIS OWN SAFETY, JUST THE FIERY FUEL OF VENGEANCE LIT BY THE CHERISHED MEMORY OF HIS FAVORITE TEACHER, THE ONLY ONE WHO BELIEVED IN HIM, WHO TOOK THE TIME AND MADE HIM FEEL AS IF HE COUNTED, WHOSE VERY WORDS RANG TRUE ENOUGH WHEN HE DOUBTED SCHOOL AND LURED HIM BACK. AND TO THIS SHE-BEAST, MS. LOCKHART WAS MERELY A MEAL ENDING UP AS DUNG!

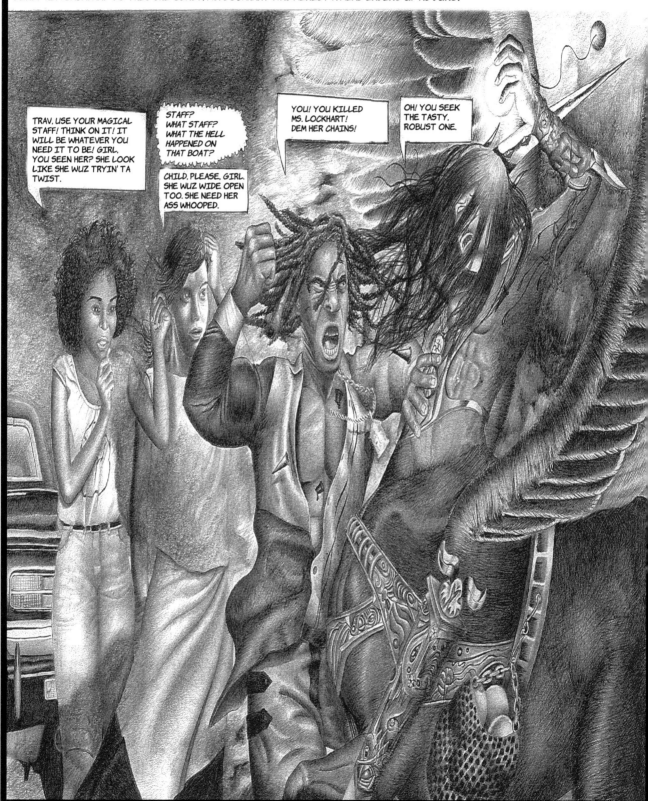

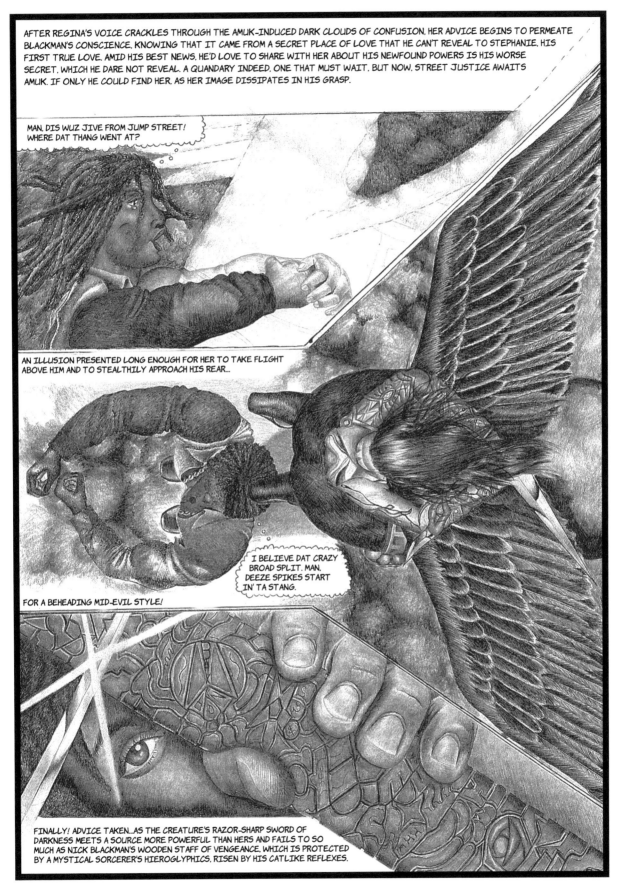

AFTER REGINA'S VOICE CRACKLES THROUGH THE AMUK-INDUCED DARK CLOUDS OF CONFUSION, HER ADVICE BEGINS TO PERMEATE BLACKMAN'S CONSCIENCE. KNOWING THAT IT CAME FROM A SECRET PLACE OF LOVE THAT HE CAN'T REVEAL TO STEPHANIE, HIS FIRST TRUE LOVE. AMID HIS BEST NEWS, HE'D LOVE TO SHARE WITH HER ABOUT HIS NEWFOUND POWERS IS HIS WORSE SECRET, WHICH HE DARE NOT REVEAL. A QUANDARY INDEED, ONE THAT MUST WAIT. BUT NOW, STREET JUSTICE AWAITS AMUK. IF ONLY HE COULD FIND HER, AS HER IMAGE DISSIPATES IN HIS GRASP.

MAN, DIS WUZ JIVE FROM JUMP STREET! WHERE DAT THANG WENT AT?

AN ILLUSION PRESENTED LONG ENOUGH FOR HER TO TAKE FLIGHT ABOVE HIM AND TO STEALTHILY APPROACH HIS REAR...

I BELIEVE DAT CRAZY BROAD SPLIT. MAN, DEEZE SPIKES START IN' TA STANG.

FOR A BEHEADING MID-EVIL STYLE!

FINALLY! ADVICE TAKEN...AS THE CREATURE'S RAZOR-SHARP SWORD OF DARKNESS MEETS A SOURCE MORE POWERFUL THAN HERS AND FAILS TO SO MUCH AS NICK BLACKMAN'S WOODEN STAFF OF VENGEANCE, WHICH IS PROTECTED BY A MYSTICAL SORCERER'S HIEROGLYPHICS, RISEN BY HIS CATLIKE REFLEXES.

SUDDENLY, A STRANGE CONNECTION HAPPENS: THE STAFF, LIKE A TREE, NEEDS THE EARTH TO LIVE. TRAV BECOMES THE EARTH FOR THE STAFF AND THE SPIRITS WITHIN HIM IS THE WATER. AND IN THE MANNER IN WHICH A TREE, NOW BEING THE STAFF, INSTINCTIVELY SURVIVES THE ELEMENTS. THE STAFF SYSTEMATICALLY BLASTS AMUK, IGNITING A SLOW BURN FROM WITHIN THE SHE-BEAST.

THE FORCE OF THE BLAST SMASHES HER AGAINST THE SCHOOL WALL IN MID-AIR, AND FOR THE FIRST TIME, AMUK EXPERIENCES PAIN WITHOUT SHEER DELIGHT WHICH IS SUBSTITUTED BY ANGER AND CONFUSION.

OUTTA SIGHT! MAN, DIS THANG IZ THROWIN' DOWN!

STILL, BLACKMAN'S RAGE IS...

PARAMOUNT AND HAS YET TO BE SUFFICED, SO HE REACHES FOR A LOOSE BRICK FROM THE FALLING DEBRIS.

AND IT BECOMES THE DEATH BLOW TO A STUNNED AND BURNING AMUK.

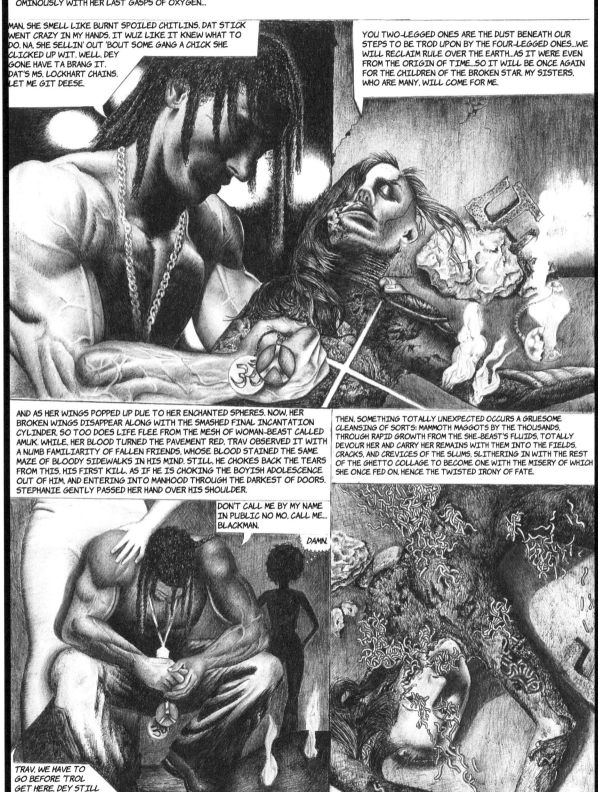

AS HER FINAL INCANTATION CYLINDER SMASHES INTO THE CONCRETE BOTTOM OF THE CAGE CALLED THE GHETTO, HER WINGS WHICH APPEARED THEN AREN'T THERE—VANISHED. BLACKMAN LEANS OVER HER TO RETRIEVE THE TWO SYMBOLS OF PEACE, WHICH ONCE BELONGED TO HIS BELOVED TEACHER, MS. LOCKHART, FROM THE NECK OF HIS ENEMY. INTERNALLY, HE QUERIES, "WHAT PEACE?" AS IF IT IS SOME FOREIGN UNATTAINABLE COMMODITY FOR ONLY THE PRIVILEGED. AMLIK'S FRIGID STARE DIMINISHES INTO NOTHINGNESS AS SHE FOREBODES OMINOUSLY WITH HER LAST GASPS OF OXYGEN...

MAN, SHE SMELL LIKE BURNT SPOILED CHITLINS. DAT STICK WENT CRAZY IN MY HANDS. IT WUZ LIKE IT KNEW WHAT TO DO. NA. SHE SELLIN' OUT 'BOUT SOME GANG A CHICK SHE CLICKED UP WIT. WELL, DEY GONE HAVE TA BRANG IT. DAT'S MS. LOCKHART CHAINS. LET ME GIT DEESE.

YOU TWO-LEGGED ONES ARE THE DUST BENEATH OUR STEPS TO BE TROD UPON BY THE FOUR-LEGGED ONES...WE WILL RECLAIM RULE OVER THE EARTH...AS IT WERE EVEN FROM THE ORIGIN OF TIME...SO IT WILL BE ONCE AGAIN FOR THE CHILDREN OF THE BROKEN STAR. MY SISTERS, WHO ARE MANY, WILL COME FOR ME.

AND AS HER WINGS POPPED UP DUE TO HER ENCHANTED SPHERES. NOW, HER BROKEN WINGS DISAPPEAR ALONG WITH THE SMASHED FINAL INCANTATION CYLINDER, SO TOO DOES LIFE FLEE FROM THE MESH OF WOMAN-BEAST CALLED AMLIK. WHILE, HER BLOOD TURNED THE PAVEMENT RED, TRAV OBSERVED IT WITH A NUMB FAMILIARITY OF FALLEN FRIENDS, WHOSE BLOOD STAINED THE SAME MAZE OF BLOODY SIDEWALKS IN HIS MIND. STILL, HE CHOKES BACK THE TEARS FROM THIS, HIS FIRST KILL. AS IF HE IS CHOKING THE BOYISH ADOLESCENCE OUT OF HIM, AND ENTERING INTO MANHOOD THROUGH THE DARKEST OF DOORS. STEPHANIE GENTLY PASSED HER HAND OVER HIS SHOULDER.

THEN, SOMETHING TOTALLY UNEXPECTED OCCURS A GRUESOME CLEANSING OF SORTS: MAMMOTH MAGGOTS BY THE THOUSANDS, THROUGH RAPID GROWTH FROM THE SHE-BEAST'S FLUIDS, TOTALLY DEVOUR HER AND CARRY HER REMAINS WITH THEM INTO THE FIELDS, CRACKS, AND CREVICES OF THE SLUMS, SLITHERING IN WITH THE REST OF THE GHETTO COLLAGE TO BECOME ONE WITH THE MISERY OF WHICH SHE ONCE FED ON. HENCE THE TWISTED IRONY OF FATE.

DON'T CALL ME BY MY NAME IN PUBLIC NO MO. CALL ME... BLACKMAN.

DAMN.

TRAV, WE HAVE TO GO BEFORE TROL GET HERE. DEY STILL LOOKING FO YOU.

33

IT'S BEEN THREE DAYS REMOVED, AND WHAT TERRIBLE THINGS THOSE WORMS ARE AND WHAT A TERRIBLE THING AMUK WAS. NOW, THAT NOTHING IS LEFT OF HER, IT'S AS IF SHE NEVER EXISTED. BUT TRAV KNOWS, THEY ALL KNOW THE CREATURE DID BECAUSE MS. LOCKHART IS GONE. STEPH LEANS ON THE WALL AS REGINA SCOLDS TRAV.

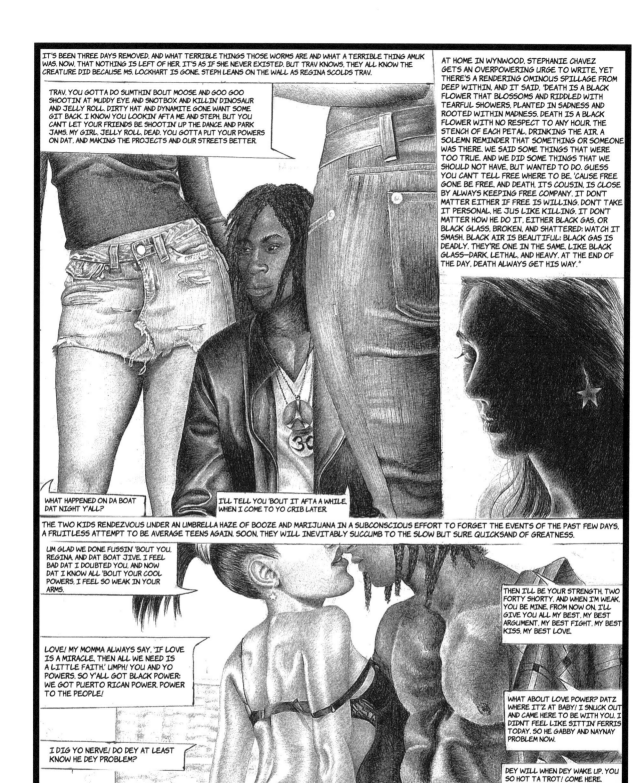

TRAV, YOU GOTTA DO SUMTHIN' BOUT MOOSE AND GOO GOO SHOOTIN' AT MUDDY EYE AND SNOTBOX AND KILLIN' DINOSAUR AND JELLY ROLL. DIRTY HAT AND DYNAMITE GONE WANT SOME GIT BACK. I KNOW YOU LOOKIN' AFTA ME AND STEPH, BUT YOU CAN'T LET YOUR FRIENDS BE SHOOTIN' UP THE DANCE AND PARK JAMS. MY GIRL, JELLY ROLL, DEAD. YOU GOTTA PUT YOUR POWERS ON DAT, AND MAKING THE PROJECTS AND OUR STREETS BETTER.

AT HOME IN WYNWOOD, STEPHANIE CHAVEZ GETS AN OVERPOWERING URGE TO WRITE, YET THERE'S A RENDERING OMINOUS SPILLAGE FROM DEEP WITHIN, AND IT SAID, 'DEATH IS A BLACK FLOWER THAT BLOSSOMS AND RIDDLED WITH TEARFUL SHOWERS, PLANTED IN SADNESS AND ROOTED WITHIN MADNESS. DEATH IS A BLACK FLOWER WITH NO RESPECT TO ANY HOUR. THE STENCH OF EACH PETAL, DRINKING THE AIR. A SOLEMN REMINDER THAT SOMETHING OR SOMEONE WAS THERE. WE SAID SOME THINGS THAT WERE TOO TRUE. AND WE DID SOME THINGS THAT WE SHOULD NOT HAVE, BUT WANTED TO DO. GUESS YOU CAN'T TELL FREE WHERE TO BE, 'CAUSE FREE GONE BE FREE, AND DEATH, ITS COUSIN, IS CLOSE BY ALWAYS KEEPING FREE COMPANY. IT DON'T MATTER EITHER IF FREE IS WILLING. DON'T TAKE IT PERSONAL, HE JUS LIKE KILLING. IT DON'T MATTER HOW HE DO IT, EITHER BLACK GAS, OR BLACK GLASS, BROKEN, AND SHATTERED; WATCH IT SMASH. BLACK AIR IS BEAUTIFUL; BLACK GAS IS DEADLY. THEY'RE ONE IN THE SAME. LIKE BLACK GLASS—DARK, LETHAL, AND HEAVY. AT THE END OF THE DAY, DEATH ALWAYS GET HIS WAY."

WHAT HAPPENED ON DA BOAT DAT NIGHT Y'ALL?

I'LL TELL YOU 'BOUT IT AFTA A WHILE, WHEN I COME TO YO CRIB LATER.

THE TWO KIDS RENDEZVOUS UNDER AN UMBRELLA HAZE OF BOOZE AND MARIJUANA IN A SUBCONSCIOUS EFFORT TO FORGET THE EVENTS OF THE PAST FEW DAYS, A FRUITLESS ATTEMPT TO BE AVERAGE TEENS AGAIN. SOON, THEY WILL INEVITABLY SUCCUMB TO THE SLOW BUT SURE QUICKSAND OF GREATNESS.

I'M GLAD WE DONE FUSSIN 'BOUT YOU, REGINA, AND DAT BOAT JIVE. I FEEL BAD DAT I DOUBTED YOU, AND NOW DAT I KNOW ALL 'BOUT YOUR COOL POWERS, I FEEL SO WEAK IN YOUR ARMS.

LOVE! MY MOMMA ALWAYS SAY, 'IF LOVE IS A MIRACLE, THEN ALL WE NEED IS A LITTLE FAITH.' UMPH! YOU AND YO POWERS. SO Y'ALL GOT BLACK POWER; WE GOT PUERTO RICAN POWER. POWER TO THE PEOPLE!

I DIG YO NERVE! DO DEY AT LEAST KNOW HE DEY PROBLEM?

CHILD, PLEASE! YO DRUNK SELF. YOU IZ OUTRAGEOUS!

THEN I'LL BE YOUR STRENGTH, TWO FORTY SHORTY. AND WHEN I'M WEAK, YOU BE MINE. FROM NOW ON, I'LL GIVE YOU ALL MY BEST, MY BEST ARGUMENT, MY BEST FIGHT, MY BEST KISS, MY BEST LOVE.

WHAT ABOUT LOVE POWER? DATZ WHERE IT'Z AT BABY! I SNUCK OUT AND CAME HERE TO BE WITH YOU. I DIDN'T FEEL LIKE SITTIN' FERRIS TODAY. SO HE GABBY AND NAYNAY PROBLEM NOW.

DEY WILL WHEN DEY WAKE UP. YOU SO HOT TA TROT! COME HERE.

WITH THE AIR OF AFTER SEX STILL STEAMING BETWEEN THE TWO TEENS, BIGOTED ANIMOSITY STARES COLDLY AT THEM FROM BEHIND, LOATHING THEIR CAREFREE EMBRACE.

WHY YOU ALWAYS THROWN MUD AT YO. FAMILY, STEY?

I MEAN, I'M NOT THROWIN' MUD AT MY FAMILY. IT'S IMPOSSIBLE TO THROW THAT MUCH MUD. ALL YOU CAN DO IS WADE IN IT. BESIDES, SOME BEAUTIFUL THINGS HAVE COME FROM MUD. WHO DON'T LOVE PORK CHOPS?

DATZ COLD, BABY.

MEANWHILE, AS TRAVALE SHIRKS HIS DUTY AS A BIG BROTHER, LOYAL SON, AND MAN OF HIS WORD TO BABYSIT HIS LITTLE BROTHER BACK AT HOME, FERRIS SLIDES UNDER HIS PRIZE-WINNING ART PIECE, IRONICALLY NAMED EVIL EYES AND SLIPS, SNEAKING PASS NAY NAY, THE LAST OBSTACLE OF SNOOZING OLDER SISTER, ON THE WAY TO THE ALL-DAY, NEWLY OPENED KIDS ROLLERTHEQUE/ DANCE SPOT JUST FOR KIDS WHERE HE HAD TO BE, NO MATTER THE COST.

TEH HEH HEH! I JUS GOT BY GABBIE. SHE NAPPIN' HARD IN THE BEDROOM, NA. IF I CAN GIT BY NAY NAY, OLD SLEEPY, BIG HEAD BUTT, I GOTTA SPLIT MAN.

AT THE SAME TIME IN WYNWOOD, STEPHANIE CHAVEZ SHIVERS IN DEAR FROM THE COLD ABSTRACT IGNORANCE, SPEWING OUTWARD FROM HER VERY OWN NEIGHBORHOOD KINSMAN.

I SEE HIS BLACKNESS IN YOUR FACE, CHICA!

¡BORICUA CHICA ESTUPIDA!

¡NOSOTROS VAMOS A MATARLO! (WE GONNA KILL HIM!)

I WONDER WHAT DEESE DUDE'S BAG IZ. I MIGHT HAVTA KNUCK WIT ALL THREE OF 'EM.

FERRIS FROLICKED GLEEFULLY AMONG HIS CHAPERONED PEERS, FORTUNATELY FOR HIM, AVOIDING MORE INQUISITIVE RIDICULE ABOUT HIS MISSING ARM, THANKS TO THE PRESENCE OF SENSITIVE PARENTS. STILL, EVEN THEIR PRESENCE IS NO MATCH FOR THE STORM LURKING OUTSIDE. A WHIRLWIND OF DEATH ENCASED IN AN UNIMAGINABLE SPECTER HUNGRILY BARRELING THEIR WAY AS THEY DANCED INSIDE. THE TWO BROTHERS SIMULTANEOUSLY FACE THEIR ENCOUNTERS SEPARATELY.

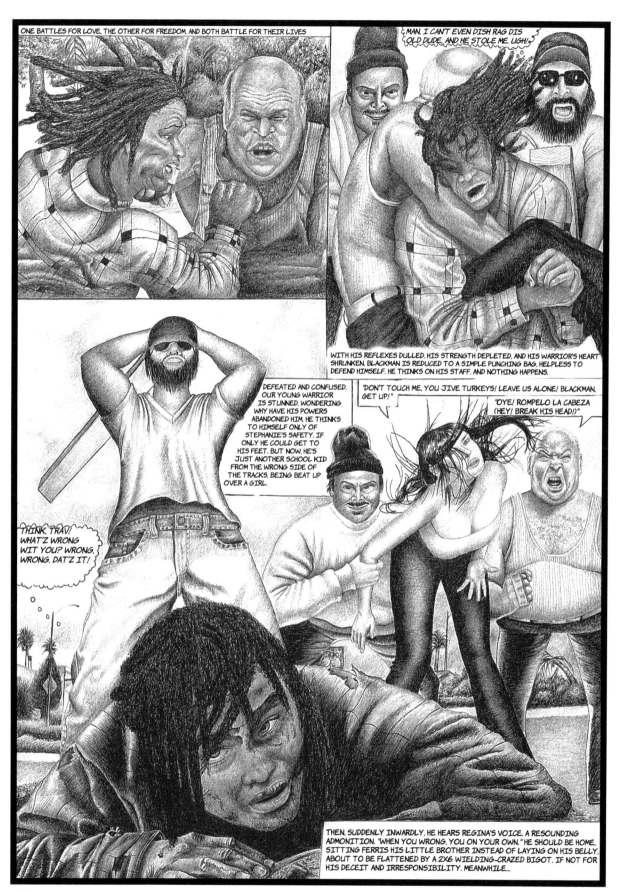

ONE BATTLES FOR LOVE, THE OTHER FOR FREEDOM, AND BOTH BATTLE FOR THEIR LIVES

"MAN, I CAN'T EVEN DISH RAG DIS OLD DUDE, AND HE STOLE ME. UGH!"

WITH HIS REFLEXES DULLED, HIS STRENGTH DEPLETED, AND HIS WARRIOR'S HEART SHRUNKEN, BLACKMAN IS REDUCED TO A SIMPLE PUNCHING BAG, HELPLESS TO DEFEND HIMSELF. HE THINKS ON HIS STAFF, AND NOTHING HAPPENS.

DEFEATED AND CONFUSED, OUR YOUNG WARRIOR IS STUNNED, WONDERING WHY HAVE HIS POWERS ABANDONED HIM. HE THINKS TO HIMSELF ONLY OF STEPHANIE'S SAFETY. IF ONLY HE COULD GET TO HIS FEET. BUT NOW, HE'S JUST ANOTHER SCHOOL KID FROM THE WRONG SIDE OF THE TRACKS, BEING BEAT UP OVER A GIRL.

"DON'T TOUCH ME, YOU JIVE TURKEYS! LEAVE US ALONE! BLACKMAN, GET UP!"

"OYE! ROMPELO LA CABEZA (HEY! BREAK HIS HEAD!)"

THINK, TRAV! WHAT'Z WRONG WIT YOU? WRONG, WRONG, DAT'Z IT!

THEN, SUDDENLY INWARDLY, HE HEARS REGINA'S VOICE, A RESOUNDING ADMONITION. "WHEN YOU WRONG, YOU ON YOUR OWN." HE SHOULD BE HOME, SITTING FERRIS HIS LITTLE BROTHER INSTEAD OF LAYING ON HIS BELLY, ABOUT TO BE FLATTENED BY A 2X6 WIELDING-CRAZED BIGOT. IF NOT FOR HIS DECEIT AND IRRESPONSIBILITY. MEANWHILE...

THE SUMMER OF '79 MEANT THE ABSENCE OF SUCH MODERN-DAY TECHNOLOGICAL PEARLS LIKE CELL PHONES, IPHONES, TEXTING, TWITTER, ETC. THEREFORE, THERE WERE NO WARNINGS FOR THE MERE SITTING DUCKS FOR VILLAINS OR THE FODDER FOR SUPERVILLAINS SUCH AS THE DANCING CHILDREN, OBLIVIOUS OF A RAPIDLY APPROACHING, AND NEWLY ENLARGED VEIN, WHO IS READY TO FEED!

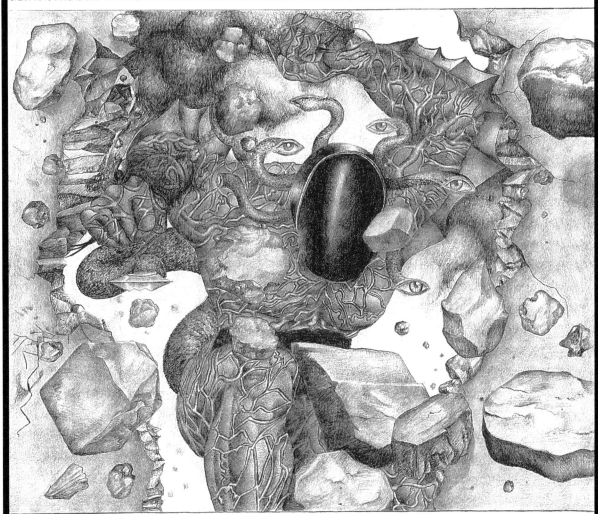

JUST LIKE LIGHT HAS A PURITY, DARKNESS HAS A PURITY. A PURE IMPURITY IN THE PUREST FORM OF DARKNESS, AND IT'S JUST AS INESCAPABLE AND EVER SO ENVELOPING. AND VEIN IS THAT PURE DARKNESS. A DARKNESS THAT WAS GIVEN BIRTH FROM A CURSED EARTH, WHO HAS BECOME DENSER AND ENHANCED IN SIZE.

YEAH! I G'ED YO STICK! NA JUMP BAD, AND BOOST YO SELF UP, TA STEP DIS WAY! O' SQUARE A—— OYE! THE BIGOTS CAN TELL BY REGINA'S

PIERCING GLARE THAT HER RESOLVE IS DEADLY. SO THEY FLEE. BUT WHERE IS FERRIS' RESCUER? WAS IT HER NEWLY ACQUIRED CLAIRVOYANCE, OR HER LOVE FILLED INTUITION THAT LED HER TO TRAV'S SIDE FIRST, OR A MATTER OF TIME WEIGHED BALANCES?

IF YOUR EYE IS DARK, HOW BRIGHT IS THAT DARKNESS? HENCE, A DARK ENERGY SEEMS TO HAVE SPAWNED FROM AN INTENTIONAL DESIRE TO DESTROY THE FUTURE. COULD REGINA HAVE MISCALCULATED HER RESCUE? WHILE YOUNG FERRIS COWERS IN HORROR AT THE SIGHT OF AN APPROACHING VEIN!

NOW WITH HIS BATTLE HAVING ENDED, BLACKMAN RECALLS THE YOUNG PROPHETESS' LAST ADMONITION CONCERNING HIS LIL BROTHER. SO HE RUNS WITH THE GIRLS IN TOW FROM 36TH STREET TO 54TH STREET WHERE REGINA JUST TOLD HIM OF FERRIS' PERIL AND WHERE HE WOULD BE.

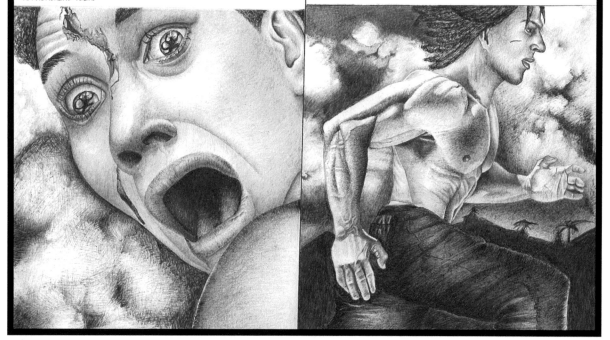

WOEFULLY, HIS TIMING WAS SHORT AND OUT, AND HIS FINDING WOULD STAGGER HIM. ALL HE COULD DO WAS DROWN IN REMORSE AND HELPLESSLY ENDURE A LIFE LESSON, WHICH WOULD BE A GUIDE POST THAT HE WILL USE FOR THE UNCHARTED PATH THAT LIES AHEAD. THE SOUL OF REGINA'S GRANDMOTHER, QUEEN ITHALIA, PUTS IT INTO WORDS AND INTO THE MOUTH OF HER FAR-REMOVED GRANDDAUGHTER, REGINA WILLIAMS, BEFORE A MAUDLIN AND STUNNED STEPHANIE CHAVEZ, WHO WITNESSED FOR THE FIRST TIME, THE SLOWLY BLOSSOMING POWERS OF REGINA THE PROPHETESS. POWERS THAT SEE THE PAST VIVID WHEN SUMMONED, PRESENT DANGERS TO A DEGREE AND KNOWLEDGE FROM THE ANCIENTS OF THE UNKNOWN, RENOWNED MASTERS OF THE ARTS

I CALLED 'TROL AND TOLD 'EM IT WUZ A SHOOTOUT AT THE ROLLER DERBY ON 54TH STREET, TO GIT 'EM TA C'MERE. I GUESS DEY DIDN'T FALL FO IT. BLACKMAN, I COULDN'T BE AT TWO PLACES AT A TIME. I MADE A MISTAKE.

DON'T TOUCH ME! I SHOULD A BEEN WATCHIN' MY BROTHA. INSTEAD A BEIN' WIT YOU! FERRIS! NOOO!

DON'T BLAME HER, BLACKMAN. IF YOU NOT GONNA DO SUMTHIN', DON'T SAY IT, AND IF YOU SAY IT, YOU HAFTA DO IT. CAN YOU SEE A SHARK'S TEARS UNDERWATER? CAN YOU COUNT THE RAINDROPS THAT IT TAKES TO WASH THESE STREETS CLEAN? IF SO, THEN YOU CAN TELL THE SPIRITS IN YOU TO DEFY THEIR PURPOSE TO AVENGE EVERY DROP OF WRONGFULLY SPILLED BLOOD THAT FLOWS INTO RIVERS OF RAGE. THE BLACK FEET OF THE WARRIOR SPIRITS OF THOSE WHO DEFIED SLAVERY, EVEN TO THE DEATH MARCH AGAINST ALL MANNER OF WRONG AND EVIL AND WILL NOT ABIDE WITH IT, THEY RISE ONLY TO AVENGE AND DESTROY IT.

THE SLAIN CHILDREN ARE STREWN ABOUT THE NAKED CONCRETE FLOOR LIKE THE MORBID FLOOR COVERING OF HADES ITSELF. DESIGNED BY AN ARCHITECT OF DEATH—VEIN!

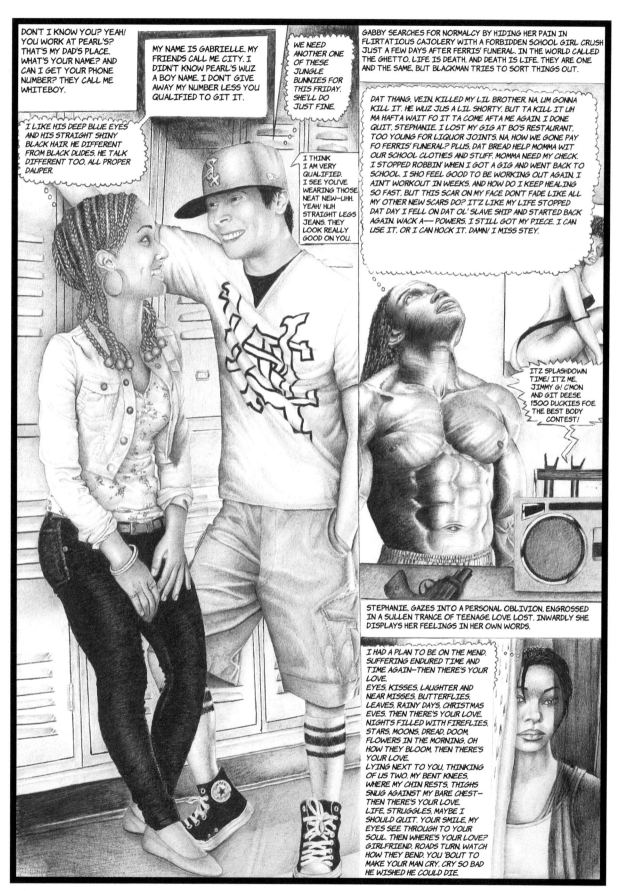

DON'T I KNOW YOU? YEAH! YOU WORK AT PEARL'S? THAT'S MY DAD'S PLACE. WHAT'S YOUR NAME? AND CAN I GET YOUR PHONE NUMBER? THEY CALL ME WHITEBOY.

MY NAME IS GABRIELLE. MY FRIENDS CALL ME CITY. I DIDN'T KNOW PEARL'S WUZ A BOY NAME. I DON'T GIVE AWAY MY NUMBER LESS YOU QUALIFIED TO GIT IT.

WE NEED ANOTHER ONE OF THESE JUNGLE BUNNIES FOR THIS FRIDAY. SHE'LL DO JUST FINE.

I LIKE HIS DEEP BLUE EYES AND HIS STRAIGHT SHINY BLACK HAIR. HE DIFFERENT FROM BLACK DUDES. HE TALK DIFFERENT TOO, ALL PROPER DAUPER.

I THINK I AM VERY QUALIFIED. I SEE YOU'VE WEARING THOSE NEAT NEW—UHH. YEAH! HUH STRAIGHT LEGS JEANS. THEY LOOK REALLY GOOD ON YOU.

GABBY SEARCHES FOR NORMALCY BY HIDING HER PAIN IN FLIRTATIOUS CAJOLERY WITH A FORBIDDEN SCHOOL GIRL CRUSH JUST A FEW DAYS AFTER FERRIS' FUNERAL. IN THE WORLD CALLED THE GHETTO, LIFE IS DEATH, AND DEATH IS LIFE. THEY ARE ONE AND THE SAME, BUT BLACKMAN TRIES TO SORT THINGS OUT.

DAT THANG, VEIN, KILLED MY LIL BROTHER. NA, LIM GONNA KILL IT. HE WUZ JUS A LIL SHORTY. BUT TA KILL IT LIH MA HAFTA WAIT FO IT TA COME AFTA ME AGAIN. I DONE QUIT, STEPHANIE. I LOST MY GIG AT BO'S RESTAURANT. TOO YOUNG FOR LIQUOR JOINTS. NA, HOW WE GONE PAY FO FERRIS' FUNERAL? PLUS, DAT BREAD HELP MOMMA WIT OUR SCHOOL CLOTHES AND STUFF. MOMMA NEED MY CHECK. I STOPPED ROBBIN' WHEN I GOT A GIG AND WENT BACK TO SCHOOL. I SHO FEEL GOOD TO BE WORKING OUT AGAIN. I AIN'T WORKOUT IN WEEKS. AND HOW DO I KEEP HEALING SO FAST. BUT THIS SCAR ON MY FACE DON'T FADE LIKE ALL MY OTHER NEW SCARS DO? IT'Z LIKE MY LIFE STOPPED DAT DAY I FELL ON DAT OL' SLAVE SHIP AND STARTED BACK AGAIN. WACK A--- POWERS. I STILL GOT MY PIECE. I CAN USE IT, OR I CAN HOCK IT. DAMN! I MISS STEY.

ITZ SPLASHDOWN TIME! IT'Z ME, JIMMY G! C'MON AND GIT DEESE 1500 DUCKIES FOE THE BEST BODY CONTEST!

STEPHANIE, GAZES INTO A PERSONAL OBLIVION, ENGROSSED IN A SULLEN TRANCE OF TEENAGE LOVE LOST. INWARDLY SHE DISPLAYS HER FEELINGS IN HER OWN WORDS.

I HAD A PLAN TO BE ON THE MEND. SUFFERING ENDURED TIME AND TIME AGAIN—THEN THERE'S YOUR LOVE.
EYES, KISSES, LAUGHTER AND NEAR MISSES, BUTTERFLIES, LEAVES, RAINY DAYS, CHRISTMAS EVES. THEN THERE'S YOUR LOVE. NIGHTS FILLED WITH FIREFLIES, STARS, MOONS, DREAD, DOOM, FLOWERS IN THE MORNING, OH HOW THEY BLOOM. THEN THERE'S YOUR LOVE.
LYING NEXT TO YOU, THINKING OF US TWO. MY BENT KNEES, WHERE MY CHIN RESTS, THIGHS SNUG AGAINST MY BARE CHEST— THEN THERE'S YOUR LOVE.
LIFE, STRUGGLES, MAYBE I SHOULD QUIT. YOUR SMILE, MY EYES SEE THROUGH TO YOUR SOUL. THEN WHERE'S YOUR LOVE? GIRLFRIEND, ROADS TURN, WATCH HOW THEY BEND. YOU 'BOUT TO MAKE YOUR MAN CRY. CRY SO BAD HE WISHED HE COULD DIE.

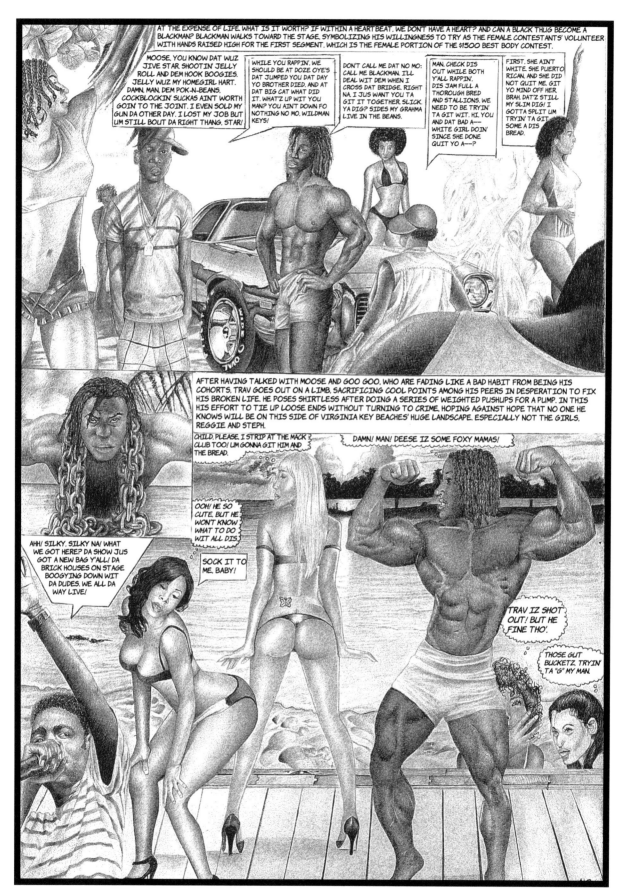

42

MOST OF THE '70S KIDS IN AMERICA WOULD BE ABLE TO ENJOY THE SPECTACLE ON STAGE, THE MUSIC, AND THE BEACH. UNFORTUNATELY, LIVING IN A QUASI-WARZONE CULTURE MEANS READINESS FOR THE INEVITABLE GUNSHOTS. YES, EXCEPT FOR THE CHILDREN FROM THE HEART OF LIBERTY CITY'S INNER CITY. A CITY WITH THE VICIOUS HEART OF A FEMALE WOLF THAT WILL HUNT AND DEVOUR EVEN HER VERY OWN PRECIOUS OFFSPRING, EVEN UP TO THE SHORES OF VIRGINIA KEY BEACH. ONE TERRIBLE HEARTBEAT IS EQUAL ALMOST IN TERROR TO THE THREE HEARTS THUDDING INSIDE OF VEIN. CAN THE LOVE BORN IN BLACKMAN'S HEART OVERCOME THOSE ODDS? SADLY, TRAVALE'S COUNSELING TO MOOSE FELL ON DEATH'S EARS FOR NOT ONLY HIM BUT ALSO MUDDY EYE'S EAR, LITERALLY. AND GOO GOO CARRIES ON WITH SOLDIERLIKE LOYALTY ALONGSIDE HIS COMRADE. KILLINGS SPAWNED TWO WEEKS AGO FROM A COINCIDENTAL BUMP IN THE DARK AT ANOTHER TEEN MENAGERIE, INNOCENTLY TITLED DISCO CITY.

A DEPRIVED SOCIETY IS THE BIRTHPLACE OF DEPRAVITY, AND LOST SOULS ARE COMMON PLACE. HENCE, THE HUNTING GROUNDS OF VEIN, TUNNELING FROM BENEATH THE SURFACE OF THE BEACH. A QUAKE TROUBLES THE GROUND. POISONOUS FUMES PIERCE THE AIR. AS THE BODIES GO UP, THE EYELASHES CLOSE PERMANENTLY SHUT THE DARK BEAST, ALMOST AS IF HE IS TAKING THE PULSE OF A COMMUNITY, ONLY LATER TO STOP IT BY TAKING THE VERY SOULS OF THOSE WHO INHABIT IT. AND TO HIS PATIENT ANTICIPATION, OUR YOUNG HERO STEALTHILY CREEPS UP BEHIND VEIN, ANXIOUS TO EXACT VENGEANCE ON THE HEAD OF HIS LITTLE BROTHER'S KILLER.

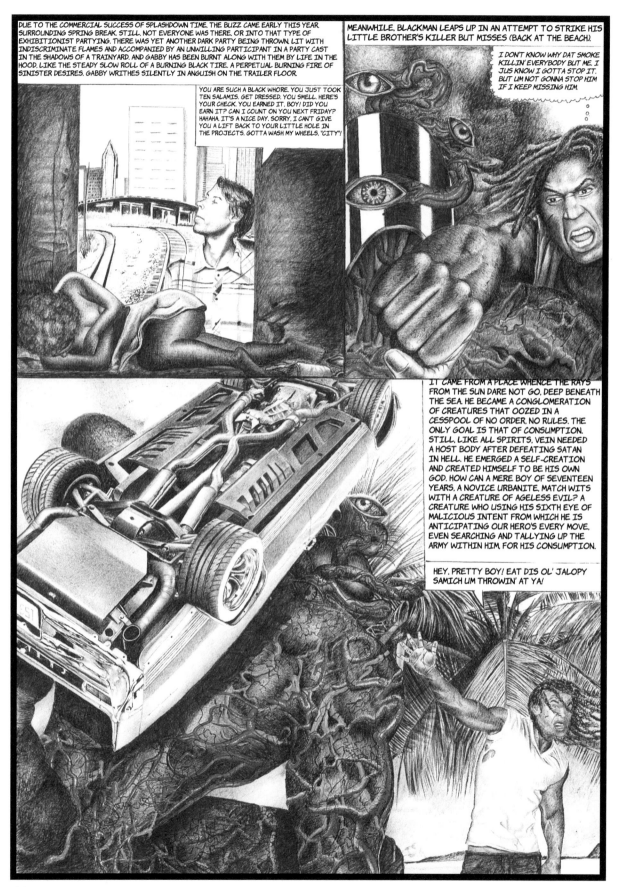

DUE TO THE COMMERCIAL SUCCESS OF SPLASHDOWN TIME, THE BUZZ CAME EARLY THIS YEAR SURROUNDING SPRING BREAK. STILL, NOT EVERYONE WAS THERE, OR INTO THAT TYPE OF EXHIBITIONIST PARTYING. THERE WAS YET ANOTHER DARK PARTY BEING THROWN, LIT WITH INDISCRIMINATE FLAMES AND ACCOMPANIED BY AN UNWILLING PARTICIPANT IN A PARTY CAST IN THE SHADOWS OF A TRAINYARD. AND GABBY HAS BEEN BURNT ALONG WITH THEM BY LIFE IN THE HOOD, LIKE THE STEADY SLOW ROLL OF A BURNING BLACK TIRE. A PERPETUAL BURNING FIRE OF SINISTER DESIRES. GABBY WRITHES SILENTLY IN ANGUISH ON THE TRAILER FLOOR.

YOU ARE SUCH A BLACK WHORE. YOU JUST TOOK TEN SALAMIS. GET DRESSED. YOU SMELL. HERE'S YOUR CHECK. YOU EARNED IT, BOY! DID YOU EARN IT? CAN I COUNT ON YOU NEXT FRIDAY? HAHAHA. IT'S A NICE DAY. SORRY, I CAN'T GIVE YOU A LIFT BACK TO YOUR LITTLE HOLE IN THE PROJECTS. GOTTA WASH MY WHEELS, "CITY"!

MEANWHILE, BLACKMAN LEAPS UP IN AN ATTEMPT TO STRIKE HIS LITTLE BROTHER'S KILLER BUT MISSES (BACK AT THE BEACH).

I DON'T KNOW WHY DAT SMOKE KILLIN' EVERYBODY BUT ME. I JUS KNOW I GOTTA STOP IT. BUT UM NOT GONNA STOP HIM IF I KEEP MISSING HIM

IT CAME FROM A PLACE WHENCE THE RAYS FROM THE SUN DARE NOT GO, DEEP BENEATH THE SEA. HE BECAME A CONGLOMERATION OF CREATURES THAT OOZED IN A CESSPOOL OF NO ORDER, NO RULES. THE ONLY GOAL IS THAT OF CONSUMPTION. STILL, LIKE ALL SPIRITS, VEIN NEEDED A HOST BODY AFTER DEFEATING SATAN IN HELL. HE EMERGED A SELF-CREATION AND CREATED HIMSELF TO BE HIS OWN GOD. HOW CAN A MERE BOY OF SEVENTEEN YEARS, A NOVICE URBANITE, MATCH WITS WITH A CREATURE OF AGELESS EVIL? A CREATURE WHO USING HIS SIXTH EYE OF MALICIOUS INTENT FROM WHICH HE IS ANTICIPATING OUR HERO'S EVERY MOVE, EVEN SEARCHING AND TALLYING UP THE ARMY WITHIN HIM, FOR HIS CONSUMPTION.

HEY, PRETTY BOY! EAT DIS OL' JALOPY SAMICH UM THROWIN' AT YA!

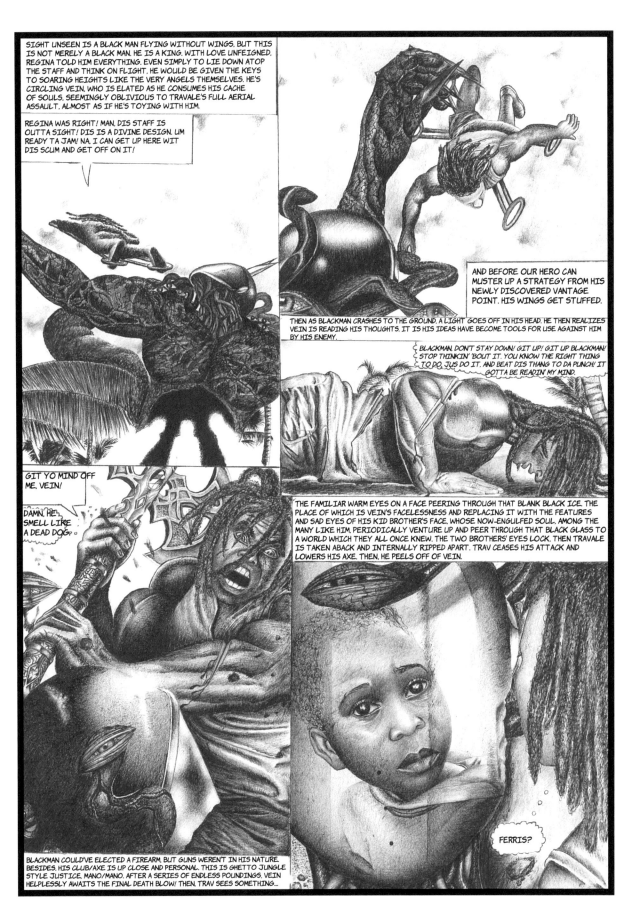

SIGHT UNSEEN IS A BLACK MAN FLYING WITHOUT WINGS, BUT THIS IS NOT MERELY A BLACK MAN. HE IS A KING. WITH LOVE UNFEIGNED, REGINA TOLD HIM EVERYTHING. EVEN SIMPLY TO LIE DOWN ATOP THE STAFF AND THINK ON FLIGHT, HE WOULD BE GIVEN THE KEYS TO SOARING HEIGHTS LIKE THE VERY ANGELS THEMSELVES. HE'S CIRCLING VEIN, WHO IS ELATED AS HE CONSUMES HIS CACHE OF SOULS, SEEMINGLY OBLIVIOUS TO TRAVALE'S FULL AERIAL ASSAULT, ALMOST AS IF HE'S TOYING WITH HIM.

REGINA WAS RIGHT! MAN, DIS STAFF IS OUTTA SIGHT! DIS IS A DIVINE DESIGN. UM READY TA JAM! NA, I CAN GET UP HERE WIT DIS SCUM AND GET OFF ON IT!

AND BEFORE OUR HERO CAN MUSTER UP A STRATEGY FROM HIS NEWLY DISCOVERED VANTAGE POINT, HIS WINGS GET STUFFED.

THEN AS BLACKMAN CRASHES TO THE GROUND, A LIGHT GOES OFF IN HIS HEAD. HE THEN REALIZES VEIN IS READING HIS THOUGHTS. IT IS HIS IDEAS HAVE BECOME TOOLS FOR USE AGAINST HIM BY HIS ENEMY.

BLACKMAN, DON'T STAY DOWN! GIT UP! GIT UP BLACKMAN! STOP THINKIN' 'BOUT IT. YOU KNOW THE RIGHT THING TO DO, JUS DO IT. AND BEAT DIS THANG TO DA PUNCH! IT GOTTA BE READIN' MY MIND.

GIT YO MIND OFF ME, VEIN!

DAMN, HE SMELL LIKE A DEAD DOG?

THE FAMILIAR WARM EYES ON A FACE PEERING THROUGH THAT BLANK BLACK ICE. THE PLACE OF WHICH IS VEIN'S FACELESSNESS AND REPLACING IT WITH THE FEATURES AND SAD EYES OF HIS KID BROTHER'S FACE, WHOSE NOW-ENGULFED SOUL, AMONG THE MANY LIKE HIM, PERIODICALLY VENTURE UP AND PEER THROUGH THAT BLACK GLASS TO A WORLD WHICH THEY ALL ONCE KNEW. THE TWO BROTHERS' EYES LOCK, THEN TRAVALE IS TAKEN ABACK AND INTERNALLY RIPPED APART. TRAV CEASES HIS ATTACK AND LOWERS HIS AXE. THEN, HE PEELS OFF OF VEIN.

FERRIS?

BLACKMAN COULD'VE ELECTED A FIREARM, BUT GUNS WEREN'T IN HIS NATURE. BESIDES, HIS CLUB/AXE IS UP CLOSE AND PERSONAL. THIS IS GHETTO JUNGLE STYLE JUSTICE, MANO/MANO. AFTER A SERIES OF ENDLESS POUNDINGS, VEIN HELPLESSLY AWAITS THE FINAL DEATH BLOW! THEN, TRAV SEES SOMETHING...

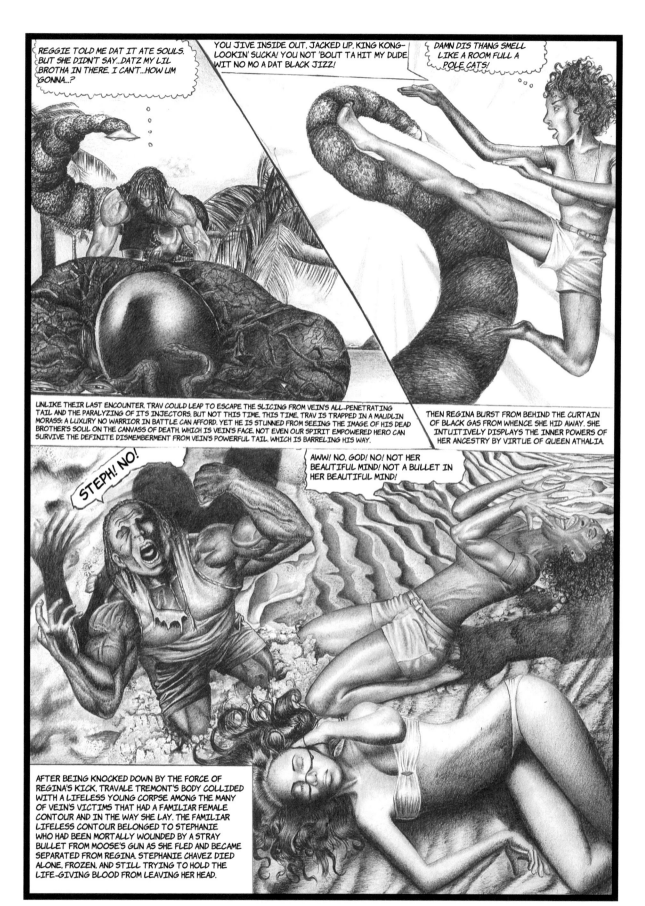

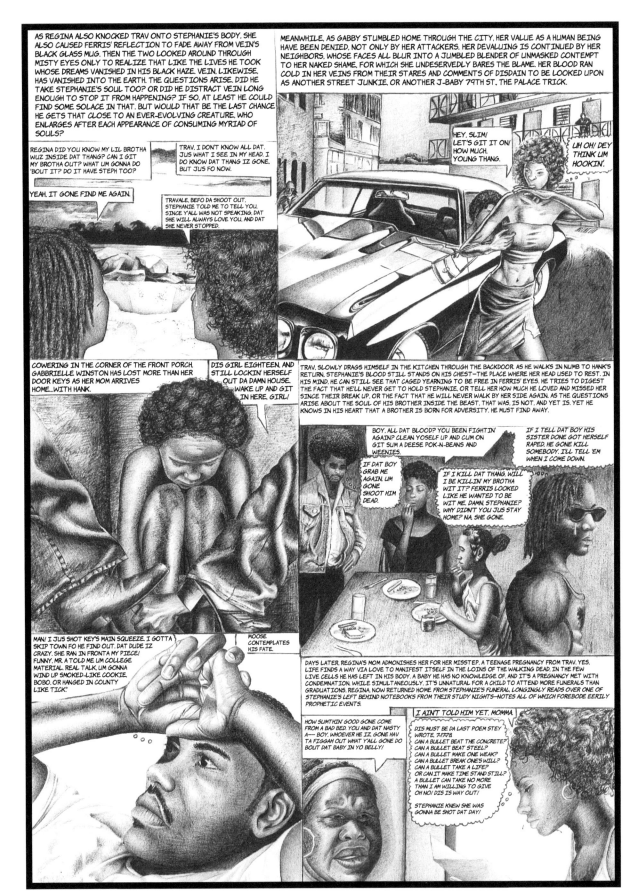

AS REGINA ALSO KNOCKED TRAV ONTO STEPHANIE'S BODY, SHE ALSO CAUSED FERRIS' REFLECTION TO FADE AWAY FROM VEIN'S BLACK GLASS MUG. THEN THE TWO LOOKED AROUND THROUGH MISTY EYES ONLY TO REALIZE THAT LIKE THE LIVES HE TOOK WHOSE DREAMS VANISHED IN HIS BLACK HAZE, VEIN, LIKEWISE, HAS VANISHED INTO THE EARTH. THE QUESTIONS ARISE. DID HE TAKE STEPHANIE'S SOUL TOO? OR DID HE DISTRACT VEIN LONG ENOUGH TO STOP IT FROM HAPPENING? IF SO, AT LEAST HE COULD FIND SOME SOLACE IN THAT. BUT WOULD THAT BE THE LAST CHANCE HE GETS THAT CLOSE TO AN EVER-EVOLVING CREATURE, WHO ENLARGES AFTER EACH APPEARANCE OF CONSUMING MYRIAD OF SOULS?

REGINA DID YOU KNOW MY LIL BROTHA WUZ INSIDE DAT THANG? CAN I GIT MY BROTHA OUT? WHAT UM GONNA DO 'BOUT IT? DO IT HAVE STEPH TOO?

TRAV, I DON'T KNOW ALL DAT. JUS WHAT I SEE IN MY HEAD. I DO KNOW DAT THANG IZ GONE, BUT JUS FO NOW.

YEAH, IT GONE FIND ME AGAIN.

TRAVALE, BEFO DA SHOOT OUT, STEPHANIE TOLD ME TO TELL YOU, SINCE Y'ALL WAS NOT SPEAKING, DAT SHE ALWAYS LOVE YOU, AND DAT SHE NEVER STOPPED.

MEANWHILE, AS GABBY STUMBLED HOME THROUGH THE CITY, HER VALUE AS A HUMAN BEING HAVE BEEN DENIED, NOT ONLY BY HER ATTACKERS. HER DEVALUING IS CONTINUED BY HER NEIGHBORS, WHOSE FACES ALL BLUR INTO A JUMBLED BLENDER OF UNMASKED CONTEMPT TO HER NAKED SHAME, FOR WHICH SHE UNDESERVEDLY BARES THE BLAME. HER BLOOD RAN COLD IN HER VEINS FROM THEIR STARES AND COMMENTS OF DISDAIN TO BE LOOKED UPON AS ANOTHER STREET JUNKIE, OR ANOTHER J-BABY 79TH ST, THE PALACE TRICK.

HEY, SLIM! LET'S GIT IT ON! HOW MUCH, YOUNG THANG.

UH OH! DEY THINK UM HOOKIN'.

COWERING IN THE CORNER OF THE FRONT PORCH, GABBRIELLE WINSTON HAS LOST MORE THAN HER DOOR KEYS AS HER MOM ARRIVES HOME...WITH HANK.

DIS GIRL EIGHTEEN, AND STILL LOCKIN HERSELF OUT DA DAMN HOUSE... WAKE UP AND GIT IN HERE, GIRL!

TRAV, SLOWLY DRAGS HIMSELF IN THE KITCHEN THROUGH THE BACKDOOR. AS HE WALKS IN NUMB TO HANK'S RETURN, STEPHANIE'S BLOOD STILL STANDS ON HIS CHEST—THE PLACE WHERE HER HEAD USED TO REST. IN HIS MIND, HE CAN STILL SEE THAT CAGED YEARNING TO BE FREE IN FERRIS' EYES. HE TRIES TO DIGEST THE FACT THAT HE'LL NEVER GET TO HOLD STEPHANIE, OR TELL HER HOW MUCH HE LOVED AND MISSED HER SINCE THEIR BREAK UP, OR THE FACT THAT HE WILL NEVER WALK BY HER SIDE AGAIN. AS THE QUESTIONS ARISE ABOUT THE SOUL OF HIS BROTHER INSIDE THE BEAST, THAT WAS, IS NOT, AND YET IS. YET HE KNOWS IN HIS HEART THAT A BROTHER IS BORN FOR ADVERSITY, HE MUST FIND AWAY.

BOY, ALL DAT BLOOD? YOU BEEN FIGHTIN' AGAIN? CLEAN YOSELF UP AND CUM ON GIT SUM A DEESE POK-N-BEANS AND WEENIES.

IF DAT BOY GRAB ME AGAIN, UM GONE SHOOT HIM DEAD.

IF I KILL DAT THANG, WILL I BE KILLIN' MY BROTHA WIT IT? FERRIS LOOKED LIKE HE WANTED TO BE WIT ME. DAMN, STEPHANIE. WHY DIDN'T YOU JUS STAY HOME? NA, SHE GONE.

IF I TELL DAT BOY HIS SISTER DONE GOT HERSELF RAPED, HE GONE KILL SOMEBODY. I'LL TELL 'EM WHEN I COME DOWN.

MAN! I JUS SHOT KEY'S MAIN SQUEEZE. I GOTTA SKIP TOWN FO HE FIND OUT. DAT DUDE IZ CRAZY. SHE RAN IN FRONTA MY PIECE! FUNNY, MR TOLD ME UM COLLEGE MATERIAL. REAL TALK, UM GONNA WIND UP SMOKED-LIKE COOKIE, BOBO, OR HANGED IN COUNTY LIKE TICK.

MOOSE CONTEMPLATES HIS FATE.

DAYS LATER, REGINA'S MOM ADMONISHES HER FOR HER MISSTEP. A TEENAGE PREGNANCY FROM TRAV. YES, LIFE FINDS A WAY VIA LOVE TO MANIFEST ITSELF IN THE LOINS OF THE WALKING DEAD, IN THE FEW LIVE CELLS HE HAS LEFT IN HIS BODY. A BABY HE HAS NO KNOWLEDGE OF, AND IT'S A PREGNANCY MET WITH CONDEMNATION. WHILE SIMULTANEOUSLY, IT'S UNNATURAL FOR A CHILD TO ATTEND MORE FUNERALS THAN GRADUATIONS. REGINA, NOW RETURNED HOME FROM STEPHANIE'S FUNERAL, LONGINGLY READS OVER ONE OF STEPHANIE'S LEFT BEHIND NOTEBOOKS FROM THEIR STUDY NIGHTS—NOTES ALL OF WHICH FOREBODE EERILY PROPHETIC EVENTS.

HOW SUMTHIN' GOOD GONE COME FROM A BAD BED, YOU AND DAT NASTY A— BOY, WHOEVER HE IZ, GONE HAV TA FIGGAH OUT WHAT Y'ALL GONE DO BOUT DAT BABY IN YO BELLY!

I AIN'T TOLD HIM YET, MOMMA

DIS MUST BE DA LAST POEM STEY WROTE, 7/7/78 CAN A BULLET BEAT THE CONCRETE? CAN A BULLET BEAT STEEL? CAN A BULLET MAKE ONE WEAK? CAN A BULLET BREAK ONE'S WILL? CAN A BULLET TAKE A LIFE? OR CAN IT MAKE TIME STAND STILL? A BULLET CAN TAKE NO MORE THAN I AM WILLING TO GIVE OH NO! DIS IS WAY OUT!

STEPHANIE KNEW SHE WAS GONNA BE SHOT DAT DAY!

BLACKMAN, THE EMBODIMENT OF CENTURIES OF UNPARALLELED PAIN ENDURED, NOW FILLED WITH THE EMBATTLED SOULS RISEN FROM DEATH, INCARNATE IN HIM TO SEEK OUT JUSTICE ON THEIR TRUE ENEMIES, HATRED, INJUSTICE AND EVIL. TRAVALE TREMONT WINSTON, OUR YOUNG MAN, SOLEMNLY INTROSPECTS ALL OF HIS KNOWN CHALLENGES. YET HIS MORE URGENT PERSONAL OBSTACLES CONCERNING REGINA'S PREGNANCY, HIS SISTER'S SEXUAL ASSAULT, AND HIS BEST FRIEND, MOOSE, HAVING BEEN THE KILLER WHO SENT THE BULLET THAT TOOK HIS FIRST LOVE, ALL HAVE YET TO BE REVEALED TO HIM. HOW CAN A FATHERLESS YOUNGSTER SUMMON THE FORTITUDE TO BARE SUCH BURDENS? CAN HE HARNESS ALL OF HIS INBRED POWERS AND USE THEM FOR GOOD DESPITE EACH DAUNTING TASK? OR WILL HE SUCCUMB TO THE SAVAGERY OF STREET VENGEANCE, AND RHETORICAL GHETTO LAWS OF SURVIVAL AND BE REDUCED TO A MERE SOULLESS WEAKLING? OR WILL HE ADHERE TO REGINA'S ADMONITION TO STAY STRONG FOR WHAT IS RIGHT. AS THE SPIRITS OF THE THREE HUNDRED WARRIORS INSIDE OF HIM, STAND AT THE READY TO BE AT HIS COMMAND, WHICH WILL HE CHOOSE? SO HANG ON HOMEBOYS AND HOMEGIRLS! IT'S GOING TO BE A BUMPY RIDE!

DAMN, I GOTTA LOOK AT DIS BUG ASS DUDE MUG SUMMO. MOMMA DONE LET THIS CREEP ASS BACK IN DA CRIB, RAPPIN' 'BOUT HOW SORRY HE IZ. SHE GONE MAKE ME HAV TO KILL DAT JIVE TURKEY IF HE BE HITTIN' HER SUM MO. PLUS, I JUS BURIED MY MAIN SQUEEZE. I DIDN'T EVEN KNOW STEY WUZ AT DA SPLASHDOWN! I GOTTA FIGAH OUT WHAT UM GONNA DO BOUT VEIN WIT ALL MY LIL BROTHA'S SOUL TRAPPED INSIDE A IT. I WISH, I COULD TALK WIT MOMMA OR SOMEBODY GROWN 'BOUT ALL DIS, BUT TO DEM UM JUS A KID. IF I TRY TO TELL DEM, DEY A JUS BLOW ME OFF. OR TURN ME OVER TO 'TROL AFTA MOMMA TRY TO BEAT ME. NAH, NUN A DAT. FORGIT DAT. UM ON MY OWN LIKE FROM DA JUMP.

AND, OH YEAH! THERE'S ALSO THAT SMALL MATTER OF THOUSANDS OF BEASTS, HALF-HUMAN, ALL FEMALE, ALL ANGRY, ALL HEADED STRAIGHT FOR EARTH, LOOKIN' FOR A DUDE CALLED BLACKMAN AND REVENGE!

BY DESTROYING AMUK, COULD BLACKMAN HAVE AWAKENED A SLEEPING GIANT? COULD THIS IMPENDING DOOM HAVE BEEN AVOIDED? OR IS THIS CENTURIES OLD CONFLICT INEVITABLE? BECAUSE THESE AIN'T SISTERS OF THE CLOTH: THEY ARE SISTERS OF THE SWORD! THEY ARE FROM LEFT TO RIGHT: AYNIA, DOMINO, INDIGO, ALPHA ZETA, STINGRAY, WILDFIRE, TEN STONES, SCORCH, EFION, NO ONE, THE OMNIPOTENT HORMAH, NIMROD, DEPRAVITY, AN INNUMERABLE HOST OF HUMAN FLESH EATERS! THEY BURY THEIR DEAD WITH THE HORSE HALF, WHICH THEY EMBRACE IN THE GROUND FOR DIGNITY, AND LEAVE THE HUMAN HALF OF THEMSELVES WHICH THEY ABHOR, EXPOSED TO THE ELEMENTS, THEN HANG ENCHANTED BEADS OF SEEING ABOUT THE NECKS OF THE CHOSEN DEAD SISTERS IN PAIRS. THESE SEEING BEADS FOR THE PRESENT MUST ONLY BE WORN BY THE DEADLIEST SISTERS OF THE PAST TO BE SEEN BY THE SISTERS OF THE FUTURE IN ORDER TO SEE INTO THE PRESENT, AND THEY ARE PRESENTLY HEADED TO EARTH TO WAGE A WAR! THE WAR OF WARS! A CONTEST THAT IS BEING CONTRIVED IN INNER DARKNESS AT THE EARTH'S CORE, RIGHT NEXT DOOR TO HELL!

THE BEADS OF SIGHT REVEAL THE DEATH OF PRIESTESS AMUCK AT THE HANDS OF THE TROUBLE SPIRITED ONE KNOWN AS BLACKMAN. BY THE BONES OF THE SISTERHOOD, THE CHILDREN OF THE BROKEN STAR WILL AT LAST LAY VENGEANCE ON THE HEADS OF THE TWO LEGGED ONES, AS THEIR TWO FEET SINK INTO THE SANDS THAT BARE THEIR FEEBLE EXISTENCE AND VANISH, SO TOO WILL THEY BE EXTINGUISHED FROM THE EARTH. FOR WE WILL UNITE THE KINGDOM OF ALL THE FOUR LEGGED ONES. BLACKMAN MUST BE MADE TO FEEL THE FULL WRATH OF HORMAH THE OMNIPOTENT, EVEN TO HIS DEATH! WE WILL AVENGE THE DEATH OF OUR SISTER! WE WILL AVENGE THE CRIES OF MOTHER EARTH FOR JUSTICE AGAINST MANKIND FOR WHAT THEY HAVE DONE TO HER!

A SWELTERING NIGHT IN THE EVER NON-AIRCONDITIONED PROJECTS KNOWN AS THE PORK-N-BEANS, WITH FAN BLADES BLAZING, SPLASHING THE SWEAT ON REGINA WILSON (ABOVE), WHO HIS TWISTING AND TURNING IN HER SLEEP. ON THE HUMID WALL BESIDE HER, HANGING ON THE WALL, IS MS. LOCKHART'S MEDALLION, A ONE-TIME GIFT FROM THE STUDENTS TO HER. IT'S NOT ONLY THE SIZZLING MIAMI SUMMER NIGHT CAUSING HER DISCOMFORT. IN HER RESTLESS SLEEP ARE WILD DREAMS SHE CAN FEEL INTENSELY. DREAMS ABOUT AMUCK, VISIONS OF SPIRITS, AND SOME HAUNTINGLY PROPHETIC POEMS ONCE WRITTEN BY HER BEST FRIEND, STEPHANIE CHAVEZ, BEFORE SHE DIED, MEMENTOS FOR KEEPSAKES THAT PROPHESY DREAD.

ONE IN PARTICULAR READ, "SEE THE WAVES HOW THEY LEAVE THE SAND AND RETURN AGAIN. SO IS LIFE OF A MAN, GENERATIONS AND DEEDS OF MANKIND. THE WAVES, HOW THEY RESEMBLE OUR CHANGING ATTITUDES, STAGES. THE WINTERS DISPLAY THE COLDNESS IN A MAN'S HEART AND LIFE AS HE AGES, AND THE STEAM FROM THE SUN THAT WRINKLES EVEN THE EARTH'S LANDSCAPES AS A MAN'S FACE, THE SUN, LIKE THEY ARE WRITING STORIES ON PAGES. OR THE WIND, HOW IT WHISTLES WHEN IT SPEAKS, WHISPERING, 'I AM HERE, THEN I'M NOT, I AM HE WHO IS THE UNSEEN INVADING EACH THOUGHT, CAPTURING EACH SECRET, BOURNE OF RAGES.'"

AND IN HER DEEP SLEEP FELL UPON HER A HORROR OF A GREAT DARKNESS APPROACH (BELOW), A DARK HORSE FROM THE DEEP OVERWHELMED BY HER JOURNEY THROUGH THE ABYSS. AMUCK IS SPARED DEATH'S SUMMONING BY A SHREW OF MERMAIDS ON HER WAY TO ADMINISTER EVIL, HENCE THE ORIGIN OF HER ARRIVAL.

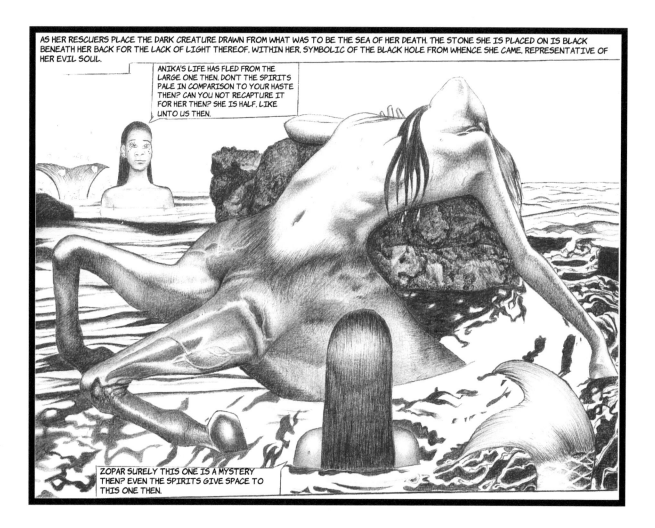

AS HER RESCUERS PLACE THE DARK CREATURE DRAWN FROM WHAT WAS TO BE THE SEA OF HER DEATH. THE STONE SHE IS PLACED ON IS BLACK BENEATH HER BACK FOR THE LACK OF LIGHT THEREOF, WITHIN HER, SYMBOLIC OF THE BLACK HOLE FROM WHENCE SHE CAME, REPRESENTATIVE OF HER EVIL SOUL.

ANIKA'S LIFE HAS FLED FROM THE LARGE ONE THEN. DON'T THE SPIRITS PALE IN COMPARISON TO YOUR HASTE THEN? CAN YOU NOT RECAPTURE IT FOR HER THEN? SHE IS HALF, LIKE UNTO US THEN.

ZOPAR SURELY THIS ONE IS A MYSTERY THEN? EVEN THE SPIRITS GIVE SPACE TO THIS ONE THEN.

SHE DREAMT...A DREAM THAT WAS SUDDENLY TURNED INTO A FIERCE REALITY, WHICH LEFT AN ENTIRE SHREW OF MERMAIDS SLAUGHTERED, TORN, AND SAVAGELY DEVOURED BY A BLOOD-DRUNK AMUCK, WHOSE SATIATED GAZE IS ALMOST HYPNOTIC LIKE A FAT TICK ON A DOG'S ASS, DRINKING BLOOD UNTIL IT BURSTS. A CHILD OF THE BROKEN STAR'S WAY OF SAYING THANKS FOR SAVING MY LIFE, LEAVING BEHIND ANOTHER CANVAS THAT SHE PAINTED BLOOD RED.

TO THE LORD OF THE TIMEKEEPERS, OR THE PROPHETS, PROPHETESS, AND SEERS, A THOUSAND YEARS IS AS ONE DAY AND ONE DAY IS AS A THOUSAN[D]
YEARS. LIKEWISE THE DREAM STATE OF OUR YOUNG PROPHETESS, WHOSE MINUTES ARE AS DAYS. AND AS SHE DREAMS, SHE ENVISIONS THE SELFSA[ME]
LIBERTY CITY STREET, SELFSAME KIDS SHE REVELS WITH. ONLY NOW, HER POWERS REVEAL NOT ONLY WHAT THEY'RE SAYING OUTWARDLY, SHE C[AN]
HEAR THEIR THOUGHTS INWARDLY AND SEES THE VERY SPIRITS THAT ARE CONTROLLING THEM. IN FACT, THESE ARE THE ACTUAL OCCURRENCES B[E]
ORCHESTRATED BY MULTIPLE EVIL SPIRITS, ALL OF WHICH HAVE SO DEEPLY EMBEDDED THEMSELVES INTO THE PSYCHE OF THEIR HOSTS THAT TH[ERE]
IS BARELY ANY SEPARATION BETWEEN THEM AND THE MANIPULATIVE EVIL SPIRITS. WHILE IN HER INESCAPABLE NIGHTMARE, REGINA HEARS THE [A]
VOICE SAY, "THERE'S SOMETHING IN THE AIR TONIGHT!" HE HAS NO IDEA JUST HOW DEATHLY CORRECT HE IS. THANK GOODNESS, OUR HEROINE'S H[EART]
ISN'T FAINT, FOR THESE FRIGHTENING, HEART-STOPPING IMAGES HAVE ONLY BEEN WITNESSED BY THE LORD'S AND HIS ANGELS' HORRIFIC MYSTE[RY]

GES. ALAS, AS THE LASCIVIOUSNESS IS PERFORMED UNDER A BLANKET OF RHYTHM THAT POUNDS HYPNOTICALLY WITH EACH DRUM BEAT. THE DJ'S TURNTABLES ST THE DECREPIT WALL (CIRCA 1979), WHICH IS DISPLAYING A PAINTED MURAL OF A MUCH IDOLIZED SON OF THE ISLES, WHO APPEARS TO BE WATCHING IN THE ROP. THE DEMONIC SPIRITS CONTINUE THEIR DOMINANCE.

CHESTRATED BY MULTIPLE EVIL SPIRITS. ALL OF WHICH HAVE SO DEEPLY EMBEDDED THEMSELVES INTO THE PSYCHE OF THEIR HOSTS THAT THERE IS BARELY ANY SEPARATION BETWEEN THEM AND THE MANIPULATIVE EVIL SPIRITS. WHILE SCAPABLE NIGHTMARE, REGINA HEARS THE DJ'S VOICE SAY, "THERE'S SOMETHING IN THE AIR TONIGHT!" HE HAS NO IDEA JUST HOW DEATHLY CORRECT HE IS. THANK GOODNESS, OUR HEROINE'S HEART ISN'T FAINT. FOR THESE FRIGHTENING, PPING IMAGES HAVE ONLY BEEN WITNESSED BY THE LORD'S AND HIS ANGELS' HORRIFIC MYSTERIES OF THE AGES. ALAS, AS THE LASCIVIOUSNESS IS PERFORMED UNDER A BLANKET OF RHYTHM THAT POUNDS HYPNOTICALLY WITH EACH DRUM DJ'S TURNTABLES AGAINST THE DECREPIT WALL (CIRCA 1979), WHICH IS DISPLAYING A PAINTED MURAL OF A MUCH IDOLIZED SON OF THE ISLES, WHO APPEARS TO BE WATCHING IN THE BACKDROP. THE DEMONIC SPIRITS CONTINUE THEIR E.

EARING LADYBUG JEANS? ABBID A— NEGRO DINOSAUR O ONE-OF-A-KIND JEANS Z. SHE GOTTA BE STILL ON WIT. PRETTY BOY HO- DA SIDE.

AIN'T STUDIN, VANESSA. DIG, GIRL. DEY GOT SOME BROAD ON SPANISH FLY. DEY CAUGHT TRYIN TO SCREW THE GEAR KNOB ON DIS RIDE AND DEY RUNNIN A TRAIN ON HER IN THE DOPE HOUSE. DEY SAY IT'Z PEE MO SISTER, FONKY SHAWN.

HONEY CHILD, PLEASE! DAT'Z WHAT SHE GIT FO ACTING LIKE A NASTY HO, WIT DEM HOT A— PANTS ALL THE WAY UP HER BOOGIE ALL THE DAMN TIME. HER AND STANK COOCHIE, PAM, BURNIN'. SHE FINA BURN ALL DEM DUDES.

GIRL, I HEARD SHE GAVE BAYBAY A BLOW JOB, AND HE HAD DA BLUE BALLS.

YO, DYNAMITE, CHECK DIS OUT! COME RIDE DIS CHOO-CHOO WE THROWIN DOWN ON! CHICK IZ WIDE OPEN, HOME-SLICE! IZ YOU DOWN FO THE GIT DOWN? GOTTA BE MO CAREFUL!

THERE'S SUMTHIN IN THE AIR TONIGHT
It Ain't Jus The Weed
SKEET SKEET SKEET
HEAD TO THE BUSHES

MAN EVERYBODY DONE GONE, AND I'M STILL HERE DEAD BROKE. MAN DIS COLD-BLOODED. DONE LOST ALL MY BREAD, SELLIN' OUT, AND KNOW I AIN'T NO GOOD AT DIS GAMBLING SH—T!

NONETHELESS, A TEENAGE GIRL ENAMORED WITH MUSIC, STYLE, AND CARS IS A PREOCCUPATION. THEREFORE, THE FASCINATION OF A TEENAGER WITH FASHION IS BOUNDLESS. EVEN IN HER VISIONS THE DIAMOND-LIKE SHINE ON THE WIRED CAR RIMS PRODUCE AN EFFECT OF DIAMOND RIMS IN HER MIND'S EYE. IN SPITE OF THE GHASTLY SPECTACLE, SOME ITEMS GAIN BRILLIANT HUES, WHILE THE PEOPLE REMAIN BLAND WITHOUT ANY SKIN-TAINTED TINT.

ALTHOUGH THE ANGELIC FLAMES OF PROTECTION SHIELD THE GHETTO KIDS FROM DIRECT SPIRITUAL INFILTRATION OF THE MALEVOLENT NATURE, THE EXTERNAL STIMULANTS CAN BE JUST AS SPELLBINDING WITH THE CHILDREN NOW HAVING BEEN SUBJECTED TO THE DISPLAYS OF ITS MAJESTICAL INCANTATIONS THROUGH HUMAN MANIFESTATIONS. THEY, THE YOUNGSTERS AND ADOLESCENTS ALIKE, WILL REMAIN EVER INFLUENCED BY THEIR DELIBERATE SPECTACLE OF POWER, AND GLORIOUS PHYSICALITY.

RATFACE WUZ TRYIN' TA SHOW OUT ON GREENMAN FINE ASS SELF. THEN HE STOLE DA MAN—SHOWBOATING, KNOWIN' HE AIN'T GONE BUST NANE GRAPE. DAT COCKY ASS DUDE CAN GIT DIS GIRL, YOU DIG.

HONEY CHILD, PLEASE. I'M SCARED A YOU. YOU IZ JUS TOO HOT TA TROT. YOU DOWN WIT DAT? BUT, YOU LIKE DEM RED CHUMPS. I DIG DEM DARK CHOCOLATE BROTHAS. SO HELFFER DON'T START NO SH——T, AND IT WON'T BE NO SH——T! 'TEH, HEH HEH.

HA, HA. HELL BITCH! I WILL DRAG YO VANILLA CHILD WANNABE ASS ALL OVER DIS PARK JAM, IF YOU TRY ME H——." "BLACK IZ BEAUTIFUL, BABY." GIGGLE, GIGGLE.

I'M A SHOW YOU HOW TA RESPECT, GREEN MAN! YOU GONE GIT RIGHT!

HMMPH!

MEAN GREEN DA BADDEST! I'M GONNA GROW UP AND FIGHT JUS LIKE GREEN MAN!

WOOO, DEY KNUCKIN' HARD, BOY!

BOOM! HE SOCKED HIM RIGHT IN DA FACE MAN!

57

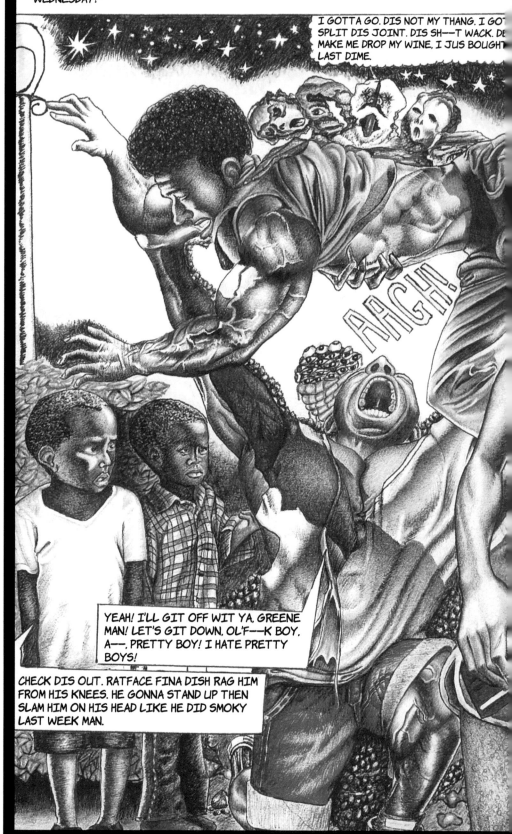

DESPITE THE AWE IN THE FACES OF THE ON LOOKERS AT THE PARKJAM, ONE CAN'T HELP BU[T]
THE UNDERTONES OF THE CROWD OF VOYEURS YOUNG AND OLD, WHO HAVE BECOME NUMB TC
WEDNESDAY?

I GOTTA GO. DIS NOT MY THANG. I GO[T]
SPLIT DIS JOINT. DIS SH——T WACK. DE
MAKE ME DROP MY WINE, I JUS BOUGH[T]
LAST DIME.

YEAH! I'LL GIT OFF WIT YA, GREENE
MAN! LET'S GIT DOWN, OL'F——K BOY,
A——, PRETTY BOY! I HATE PRETTY
BOYS!

CHECK DIS OUT. RATFACE FINA DISH RAG HIM
FROM HIS KNEES. HE GONNA STAND UP THEN
SLAM HIM ON HIS HEAD LIKE HE DID SMOKY
LAST WEEK MAN.

REGINA'S DREAM STATE VISIONS HAVE BECOME SO VIVID THAT EVEN THE FULLNESS OF THE MOON BECOMES APPARENT REVEALING THE SEETHINGLY DISGUSTING E
THE NIGHT CAN BE, UNDER THE GUISE OF A FULL MOON WHILE THE MIGHT OF RAT-FACE BOY DOMINATES GREENMAN, WHO'S BEING SLAMMED DOWN HARD, HELPLESSLY
ANYTHING THAT IT LANDS ON. THE SPECTATORS THINK THEY'RE WITNESSING A HARD THROWDOWN! AHH, BUT THERE'S MORE, MUCH MORE THAN THE NATURAL EYE CAN S

IT WAS A FULL MOON. SOMETIMES, WHEN IT WAS ORANGISH/RED, WE CALLED IT A BLOODMOON. WE'D SAY IT WAS FULL OF EVIL SPIRITS. C
THIS NIGHT, THE MOON HUNG LOW, SO I GUESS YOU KNOW...

MORE, BYSTANDERS ARE ALL ATTENTIVELY GAWKING TO CATCH A GLIMPSE OF THE ACTION. SOME ARE STREET HARDENED AND NUMBED
...ACT THAT THEY ARE WITNESSING MORE THAN A MERE SKIRMISH—THEY ARE WITNESSING A MURDER. THE GOADING OF THE INVISIBLE
...ORLD REMAINS VISIBLE ONLY TO REGINA'S MIND'S EYE, WHO HERSELF ALONE IS WITNESSING DEPLORABLE CREATURES THAT RELISH
... THE SLUDGE OF EVIL.

RATFACE WALKS AWAY, TURNING HIS BACK TO A VERY DEAD GREENMAN. THE TWO GIRLS ARE A STONE'S THROW BEHIND THE CHEVY HE WAS THROWN ONTO, CRINGE, AS RATFACE APPROACHES. WHILE THE MUSIC IS STILL THUMPING THROUGH THE TREES, WHICH LIKEWISE HAVE MOTIONLESS SUMMER LEAVES, THE '70S KIDS JUKE ON, AWARE OF THE FIGHT, BUT IGNORANT TO THE SLAYING AT THE BURNING HANDS OF RAGE PER JAMES ASH, INFAMOUSLY KNOWN AS RATFACE, WHO RECALLS HIS MOST RECENT STATE, THRUSTING G MAN ATOP THE '56 CHEVY TO HIS DEATH AND HIS MOST DISTANT RECALL OF HIS TRAGIC CHILDHOOD.

HA HA

HEE HEEHEE

GIT OUT DA WAY, KAT. HE COMIN' DIS WAY. DAT JIVE TWENTY RATFACE GOT HIM SUM COLD-BLOODED BAD SPIRITS IN HIM CHILD.

I KNOW, DAT'Z RIGHT. HE CLOCKED G-MAN A— AND STRUTTIN' OVER HIM. BUT MONA, YOU SO AWKY. AIN'T NO SUCH THANG AS SPIRITS, GIRL. STOP TRIPPIN' OUT. WHOO, HERE HE COME, GIRL. LET ME GIT OVER HERE IN THE CUT.

WHY I CAN'T MAKE NO FRIENDS, AND EVERYBODY KEEP PICKING AT ME? I CAN'T HELP THE WAY I LOOK.

NONCHALANTLY, ABOVE THE FRAY AND THE DEAFENING MUSIC, THE NAIVE YOUNG GIRLS DISCUSS THE PLAUSIBILITY OF THE SPIRIT WORLD, A CONCLUSION THAT GIVES THE SPIRITS AMUSEMENT FOR THEIR GULLIBILITY.

MOMMA LOOK AT ME. I STAND HERE, BLOODY HANDED. I NEVER THOUGHT I'D SEE THIS DAY. I LOVE. ALTHOUGH YOU NEVER SAW ME DEMAND IT, INSTEAD I WAS TREATED LIKE SH––T AND A LIFE JUST LIKE A BANDIT. I NEVER HAD A FRIEND THAT I COULD TAKE FOR GRANTED BECAUSE OF ALL THE BAD SEEDS IN ME THAT HAVE BEEN PLANTED. HERE I STAND, MOMMA, ALL BLOODY HANDED.

DON'T UNDERSTAND IT. ALL I WANTED WAS A LITTLE BITTERLY REPRIMANDED. NOW, I'M A THIEF, STEALING

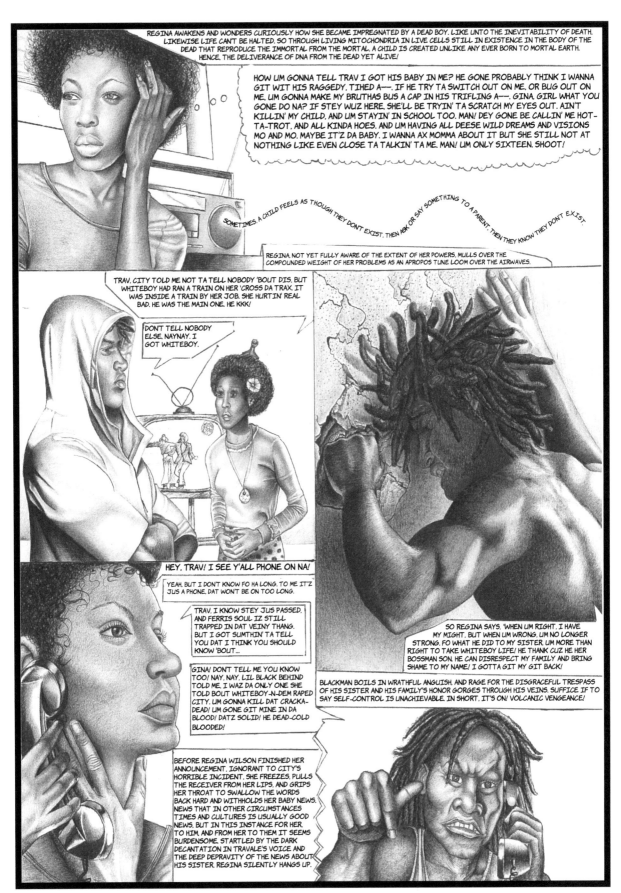

THE THING ABOUT VISIONS IS THEY CAN'T BE TOLD WHEN OR HOW TO APPEAR. THEY JUST DO! REGINA'S THIRD EYE HAS BECOME SO ACUTE THAT SHE CAN SEE A VISION AND COMMUNICATE WITH IT INTERNALLY, SIMPLY BY THINKING ON IT, AND IT REVEALS WIG LADY. REGINA CALMLY AND MENTALLY CHATS WITH WIG LADY WHO CHOKES, HANGS, STABS, RIPS APART, BRAKES ASUNDER, AND STOMPS LIKE BUGS ALL WOULD BE ESCAPEES, ONLY TO BE SCRAPED UP AND THEN THROWN BACK INTO HER WIG. EACH ONE A VEIN EFFORT TO FLEE THE MELEE FROM HER TWISTED MENAGERIE OF CURLS, WHICH ARE LIVE CURLS OF HAIR MINDFUL OF EVERY ESCAPE ATTEMPT TO WIT THERE IS NO ESCAPE. WHILE SIMULTANEOUSLY ENVISIONING THE SOON TO BE FATHER OF HER CHILD BRUTALLY BLUDGEONING HIS SISTER'S ASSAILANT, WILL WHITEBOY SURVIVE BLACKMAN? OR WILL BLACKMAN DESTROY HIMSELF WITH BLIND VENGEANCE? REGINA'S DUAL DILEMMA UNFOLDS IN HER MIND'S EYE ALL REGARDLESS OF THE BACKDROP. SHE'S STILL A LITTLE, BIG GIRL WHO CRAVES LOLLIPOPS, ANNIE B'S LIL BLACK PEARL, ANOTHER LIL GIRL WITH A BABY, OR ANOTHER BABY BY A LIL GIRL, WEARING PONYTAILS AND BOBBYSOCKS. SO REGINA ASKS HER AS SHE MARVELS_

HOW MANY PEOPLE YOU GOT IN YO HEAD?

HOW MANY PEOPLE YOU GOT IN YO HEAD?

WHY YOU WON'T LET THEM GO?

WHY WON'T YOU LET THEM GO!

WHEN YOU GONE LET THEM PEOPLE IN YO HEAD GO?

WHEN YOU GONE LET DEM OUT YO HEAD?

WIG LADY ABOUT IZ YOU EVER GONE LET DEM OUT?

IZ YOU EVER GONE LET DEM OUT YO HEAD LIL GIRL?

YOUR SISTER WAS TOO HOT A TA TROT. I JUS COULDN'T PASS IT UP, BRO! NOW EAT DIS STEEL! YA DIG? BLACKMAN!

I'M GONE BREAK ALL YO BONES, WHITEBOY!

DAMN! WHY Y'ALL ALWAYS AT DA BLACKMAN NOSE? DON'T MATTER I,M GONE SQUEEZE YO HAND 'TIL YOU BLEED, AND BRAKE YO BACK, THEN YOU GONE KNOW WHAT IT'Z LIKE TO NEED.

I COULD KILL HIM SO EASY, BUT I DON'T WANNA LOSE MY MIGHT. I GOTTA ALWAYS DO WHAT'Z RIGHT. BUT IF HE LEAVE ME NO CHOICE, HE DEAD!

DAMN! HE JUS MISSED MY NOSE! HE DEAD!

TURN ME A LOOSE, YOU BLACK NIGGER! UGH! MY FREAKING HAND, IT'S BLEEDING!

I JUS WOKE UP WIT DIS STAR UNDER MY EYE AND I,M NOT ONLY SEEING VISIONS, NA, I DONE STARTED TALKIN WIT DEM, GIRL, YOU SHO NUFF FLIPPED OUT NA, DAMN, I WISH TRAV A JUS SLOW DOWN.

About the Author

Growing up in utter impoverishment. In a sublimed section of hell fondly tagged Drew Projects, hence a namesake in the rattled ripple of the school district, in Miami. Literally cut off from benign civility, and the rest of the world, roughly translated-the belly of the whale. A seed was planted in him, that was to be conceived during his inevitable descent deeper into the belly of the whale, which was the flip side of the same coin, 18 years in prison. There he sat on prison lockers. There he rolled back thin cushioned menageries, called bedrolls, that uncovered cold hard metal slabs, which became his desk and workstation. There he waged a battle with unruly run-down pencils and the shavings thereof, that were shorn with dull makeshift razors to produce pinpoint tips. There he fought seemingly legions of inmates and guards for lighting, just to finalize a page, a section, in his effort to reduce the darkness within the belly of the whale. It was there he gave birth in the rank seepage of a poverty-stricken existence to what is soon to be known as, Tales from the belly of the whale. Don't be afraid of the dark, hence: *The Inextinguishable Dark Flame of Blackman!*